Subterranean Rome

Ivana Della Portella

Subterranean Rome

Photographs
Mark E. Smith

KÖNEMANN

© 1999 Arsenale Editrice, Venice, Italy
Designer: Giorgio Montolli

Original title: Roma sotterranea

© 2000 for this English edition:
Könemann Verlagsgesellschaft mbH
Bonner Strasse 126, D-50968 Cologne

Translation from Italian: Caroline Higgitt
in association with Goodfellow & Egan
Editing: Rose Shaw-Taylor in association with
Goodfellow & Egan.
Typesetting: Goodfellow & Egan
Project Management: Jackie Dobbyne for
Goodfellow & Egan Publishing Management,
Cambridge, UK
Production: Ursula Schümer
Printing and Binding: Neue Stalling, Oldenburg
Printed in Germany

ISBN 3-8290-2120-8

10 9 8 7 6 5 4 3 2

Photographic references:
Photographic archive *Forma Urbis*, Rome,
pp. 28, 31, 34, 39, 50, 82, 95, 105, 142, 152, 160,
162, 170, 182, 208, 220, 224–227, 228, 240, 244,
247, 262
Photographic archive, Palazzo Massimo, Rome,
pp. 166, 233
Scala photographic archive, Florence,
pp. 161, 234–235, 249, 250–251
Photographic archive of the Benedictines, Rome,
pp. 102–107, 212–215
Biblioteca Nazionale Marciana, Venice
pp. 10, 58, 62, 79, 109, 110, 112, 134
Humberto N. Serra, Rome, pp. 10, 11, 12-13
National Institute for the Graphic Arts, Rome,
p. 159
Pino Agostini, Verona, pp. 108, 111, 113

*The author wishes to thank the following for their
help:*
Father Domenicani Irlandesi, S. Clemente, Rome,
pp. 42–49, 186–193
The Carmelite Fathers of S. Martino ai Monti,
Rome, pp. 194–197
The Passionate Fathers of SS. Giovanni e Paolo,
Rome, pp. 198–205

To my mother

Contents

Foreword

The exploration of hidden Rome can start in any part, and extend in any direction, of the city, living or sleeping. There is the secret Rome of ancient houses, a treasure chest rarely revealed to the public gaze. There is the Rome of courtyards and cloisters, of hidden gardens shut away behind ancient (and modern) walls; the Rome of sacred places unexplored, abandoned or reserved for spiritual meditation and prayer. But most astonishing of all is the Rome, as vast as the visible city, that lies below the ground.

Ivana Della Portella, with her unique knowledge of, and affectionate familiarity with the city, is our guide through the familiar and unfamiliar areas of subterranean Rome. A large part of ancient Rome lies beneath our feet, often covered by the water courses that sometimes pass right over the ancient city – as is the case, for example, at the Circus Maximus – but which more frequently run through it with an intricate network of interconnected lakes, springs and little water courses; often not channeled into the ancient or modern drainage systems, and supplied by the overflowing Tiber and the sources that flow into it from all over the city.

Today the importance of archaeological research as an essential contemporary science is reinforced by new and impressive excavations. In the area of the Imperial Fora, the Commune of Rome has initiated excavations over an area equivalent to 14,000 square meters.

On the Oppian Hill, following the discovery of those charming decorations that inspired the grotesques of Renaissance decoration, we are now discovering the extraordinary architectural and artistic creations which are remnants of everyday life and which chronicle the ups and downs of the golden age of the Empire. Ivana Della Portella shows us what, today, there is to explore. She opens our eyes and our imaginations to what can be discovered, enabling us to hand on to future generations the knowledge of how much still remains in the depths of the Eternal City.

FRANCESCO RUTELLI
Mayor of Rome

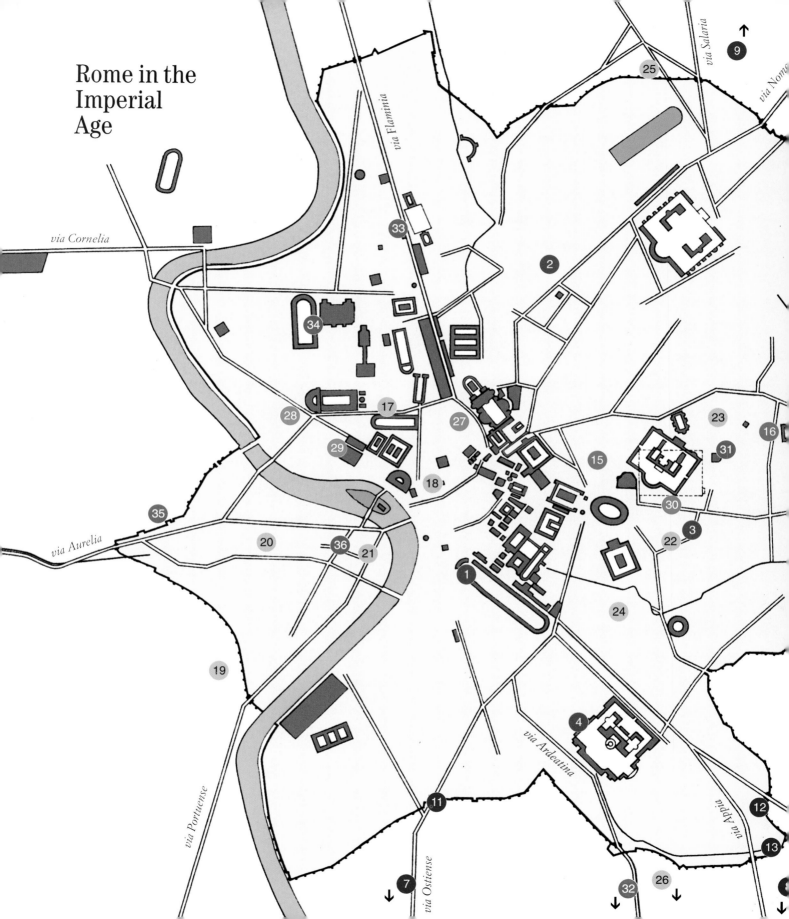

Rome in the
Imperial
Age

via Cornelia

via Salaria

via Nomen[...]

via Flaminia

via Aurelia

via Portuense

via Ostiense

via Ardeatina

via Appia

9

25

2

33

34

28

17

27

29

18

35

20

36

21

15

23

16

31

30

22

3

24

19

1

4

11

12

13

7

32

26

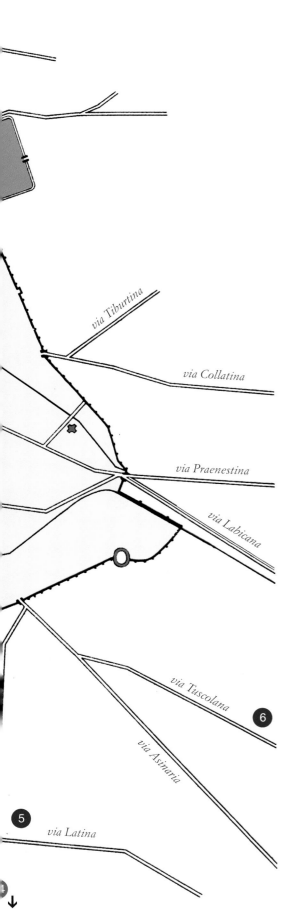

KEY

 1 Mithraeum of the Circus Maximus
 2 Barberini Mithraeum
 3 Mithraeum of S. Clemente
 4 Mithraeum of the Baths of Caracalla
 5 Tombs in the Via Latina
 6 Monte del Grano
 7 Necropolis on the Via Ostiense
 8 Mausoleum of Romulus
 9 Mausoleum of Lucilius Peto
10 Mausoleums of S. Sebastiano
11 Pyramid of Caius Cestius
12 Colombarium of Pomponius Hylas
13 Colombaria of Vigna Codini
14 Nympheum of Egeria
15 Nympheum of the Annibaldi
16 Auditorium of Maecenas
17 *Area sacra* of the Largo Argentina
18 Three temples in the Forum
   Holitorium
19 Syriac sanctuary on the Janiculum
20 S. Crisogono
21 S. Cecilia in Trastevere
22 S. Clemente
23 S. Martino ai Monti
24 SS. Giovanni e Paolo
25 Hypogeum in the Via Livenza
26 Hypogeum of the Flavians
27 Aracoeli *insula*
28 Roman house beneath the Barracco
   Museum
29 Constructions beneath S. Paolo alla
   Regola
30 *Domus Aurea*
31 *Sette Sale*
32 Roman cistern in the Via Cristoforo
   Colombo
33 Sundial of Augustus
34 Stadium of Domitian
35 Latrine in the Via Garibaldi
36 VII cohort of guards

*Right and facing:
fragments of the* Forma
Urbis, *the marble map of
Rome (scale: 1/246) that
showed the topography of
the city at the time of
Septimus Severus with
great precision. It
consisted of 11 rows of
slabs, making up a total of
151 slabs, with a width of
18.10 m. and a height of
13 m. Today only about a
tenth of the total area of
235 sq.m. survives.*

Below: fragments of the
Forma Urbis *in an
engraving by Giovanni
Battista Piranesi
(1720–1778).*

Introduction

The Rome that stands above ground beguiles us with its wealth of colors and prospects. Its sky is no ordinary sky, and its panoramas are like the stage wings and backdrops of a city that is its own theater, with its outline of cupolas, obelisks and fountains. But beneath these monuments to different centuries and styles there is another Rome, made up of ordinary, everyday things which, while certainly less spectacular than the archaeology above ground, lie buried and, for the most part, unknown. And yet, below the city, there is a rare spectacle of light and color that makes this "under" world quite unique.

Here is a labyrinth of testimonials to the past, and to past civilizations that have left colossal structures with arches, temples, columns, still protruding in places through the surface above. Hidden beneath the covering of land and time, another Rome, perhaps less grand or picturesque but no less fascinating and evocative, is discovered. Here, all the wealth and *vulgaritas* of daily life seeps from the stones.

It is a world that is ready to be explored, revealing in places a sophisticated artistic language every bit as important as those above ground. It is a journey – to borrow a phrase from Tertullian speaking of the sanctuaries to Mithras – into the kingdom of the shades (*castra tenebrarum*) to seek

Following pages: model of Rome during the Empire.

out the roots of a buried, or partially uncovered, civilization; a civilization that, for the most part, was once visible above ground, but which has been buried by the deposits of centuries.

The story is told by the *mithraea*, *columbaria*, warehouses, barracks and *hypogeia*, marking the stages of a journey that is a long way from the cultivated Latin of the Fora, revealing instead a more colloquial language that tells of the needs and beliefs of everyday life, revealing sometimes "unusual" superstitions and rituals that were hidden away or relegated to this underground world.

It is possible to trace the remains of rich *domus* and modest *insulae*, service areas and temples, offering an endlessly varying panorama with an almost infinite range of settings and contexts. In the mithraeum under the Circus Maximus, for example, it is possible to find traces of one of the most ancient eastern cults. It is not difficult to imagine the worshippers in procession to the rhythmical sound of the *tintinnabulum* or going through the harsh rituals of the initiation ceremonies. Wandering through the broad arcades of the Stadium of Domitian, a locker-room world of competitive games, in which people of all classes mingled, is evoked. In the columbarium of Pomponius Hylas an ancient vision of the afterlife is revealed in the Orphic mysteries whose graceful depiction of the underworld reduces the shadows of death to a comic theater of stuccoes and bright colors. In the Via Livenza the unsettling alchemy of

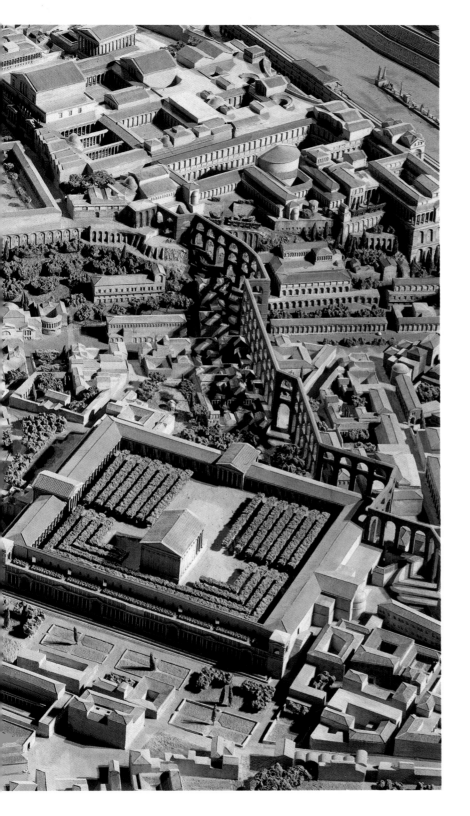

an embryonic Christianity and the last gasps of paganism can be experienced. It is difficult to say in this context whether the small basin at the back of the room was intended for the peaceful and sober ceremonies of the Christians' first ablutions, or whether it catered for the immersion of the self-styled and shameless acolytes of the *Baptai*.

In contrast, beneath S. Paolo alla Regola, we find the colors and smells of a commercial district, with its humble and shabby *insulae*. In Trastevere we find traces of the daily duties of the guard, with their barracks (*excubitorium*), and we learn from the graffiti on the walls, like a whispered legacy from the past, of rumors and fears, of tallow torches, of *siphones*, of the scarcity of water, and of an ancient and terrible monster – fire.

Our journey, which cannot hope to embrace the whole of the vast and varied panorama of subterranean Rome, tries instead to offer a representative and revealing cross-section. The approach is scholarly and scientific, but not unduly technical, so that the quality of information does not detract from an emphasis that could be described as subliminal – in other words, capable of bringing up from the darkness of the past the voices that still echo from the stones buried beneath the thick layers of the centuries.

MITHRAISM

Christianity was just becoming established when Mithraism, with its strong emphasis on the Mysteries, revived the fortunes of a declining paganism.

From their earliest appearance, these two monotheistic religions demonstrated many common points: both using rituals and liturgies with redemptive and cathartic elements, the one aiming at a broad and ecumenical audience, the other intended exclusively for a small elite of initiates. This difference was crucial, and sealed the fate of Mithraism, with its exclusive, mystical and esoteric character, through the centuries.

The spread of Mithraism

Originating in Persia, the cult took its name from the Indian and Persian god, Mithras. Always identified in the East with the sun, he was the guarantor of pacts between tribes, the god of oaths, of contracts and of all those forms and conventions of daily life that ensure peace and stability in agricultural settlements[1].

These attributes began gradually to transform him, even in ancient Persia, into a more warlike and military figure, and it is in this new guise that Mithras was to prevail as the religion spread throughout the Roman Empire. When Mithraism arrived in Greece, thanks to the good offices of some Cilician pirates[2] deported on the orders of Pompey (67 BC), it was immediately well received, due to its initiatory and redemptive character, and quickly spread throughout the Mediterranean and into northern Europe.

In the west, Mithraism took on a new character very different from its original eastern form. Through a complicated process of development, the original Zoroastrian (or Mazdean) elements of the Persian and Indian religion were replaced by later Chaldaean and Babylonian doctrines and liturgies, and more specifically by astrology, astralism and the magico-religious disciplines of Magusai sects. Roman Mithraism was the result of a syncretic process that endowed the god Mithras with very different attributes from those of the original, in whom the mystical and redemptive aspects had prevailed. The cult reached its peak in the third century AD[3], and was subsequently overtaken by the spread of Christianity at the end of the fourth century, coinciding with the decline of the Roman Empire in the west.

The myth of Mithras

In order to understand the language of the sacred images of the mithraic sanctuaries and interpret the many painted or stucco figures found in the caves dedicated to the Persian god, we need to know the myth.

One day, Mithras, a young and beautiful god, appeared as light out of the solid vault of the sky: *invictus de petra natus*[4]. The rock that had given him life put him down on the banks of a river, under the shade of a sacred tree. Some shepherds witnessed this miraculous birth. They saw him rise out of the rock naked, armed with a knife, a torch in his hand and a Phyrigian cap on his head. They gave him shelter, offering gifts and worshipping him. From the moment of his birth, Mithras began his heroic deeds that sought to subjugate the evil of the cosmos.

He began by challenging the Sun who, defeated, struck up a pact of alliance with him and passed to him his radiant crown, henceforth to be one of Mithras' attributes. Next came the story of the wild bull. Mithras captured the bull and led it into his cave (*specus*), a task that was made more difficult by the numerous obstacles set in his path (*transitus*)[5]. The bull managed to escape, however, and was seen by the Sun who sent an order to Mithras by his messenger, the Raven, to kill it. Reluctantly, Mithras undertook the task. He set off after the bull, helped by his faithful dog. As the bull was about to take shelter in the cave from which it had escaped, the god seized it by the nostrils and plunged his knife into its side (*tauroctonia*). Then from the side of the dying bull there miraculously sprang all the beneficial plants that were to inhabit the earth: from its spine came wheat and from its blood the vine. Ahriman, god of Evil, unable to stand passively by in the face of this profusion of life, sent his evil attendants, the scorpion and the snake, to fight the spread of these life-giving forces. But his attempts were in vain, and neither managed to prevent the bull's seed from

being shed on the earth, which, aided by the Moon, gave rise to every species of useful animal. Mithras and the Sun sealed their victory with a feast (*agape*), and then, climbing into the Sun's chariot, ascended to the heavens from where Mithras continued to look after the faithful.

The Mithraic cave

The cult of Mithras took place inside caverns, natural or artificial caves (*specus*).

This choice of dark and gloomy places, apart from any fascination for the awesome and the mysterious, answered a precise symolic need, as the following passage from Porphyry makes clear: "It was Zoroaster who first dedicated to Mithras, father of all things, a natural cave situated in the nearby mountains of Persia […], the cave was for him the image of the cosmos of which Mithras is the demiurge, and the objects placed in it at carefully calculated intervals were symbols of the cosmic elements and the

Mithraeum of the Circus Maximus. Triclinium used for the agape (the sacred banquet) with benches for the adepts around the edges. The large arched area at the back would have contained the main niche in which the sacred effigy with the taurorctonia *stood.*

regions of the sky[6]. The mithraic cave was, then, chosen for astrological reasons, as an allegory of the cosmos. Porphyry writes: "It was fitting that the people of ancient times dedicated caverns and caves to the cosmos [...] since for them the earth symbolized the matter which made up the cosmos [...], and, moreover, caves represented for them the cosmos that is formed by matter"[7]. We can discard Tertullian's scornful description of the mithraeum as "the kingdom of the shades" (*castra tenebrarum*)[8] – contrasting them with the *castra lucis* of the Christians – where diabolical and blasphemous rituals were performed in a kind of evil distortion of Christian rites. "And this they call Mithras, celebrating his liturgy in hidden caves, where, deep in the darkness and obscurity, they can escape the benediction of the bright sun [...] oh detestable invention of a barbaric cult!"[9]. Such invective from the Christian apologists reveals an ignorance of the significance of the choice of such sanctuaries, which emphasized the contrast between Mithras as Sun-god and his dark, subterranean place of worship. Mithras *invictus de petra natus* was born, in fact, on the day of *natalis solis* (25 December). He assumed the radiant crown and main life-enhancing virtues of the Sun, with whom, as we have seen, he had struck up a close alliance, becoming in effect a Sun-god himself. Why then would he choose the oppressive and shadowy darkness of underground caves for his cult?

The choice is less contradictory than it first appears. As Porphyry makes clear, the mithraic caves had a precise symbolic meaning, making clear allusion to the cosmos and the movement of its planets. Although it appears to have been overlooked by its Christian opponents, this symbolism was fundamental to Mithraic

thought, deeply imbued as it was with Chaldaean and Babylonian astrological ideas. Mithraism was a fusion of many elements, and could be understood on many different levels. From the dawn of the cult, it gradually moved towards a more complex form of astrological exegesis reserved for a select number of the highest grade of initiates.

Astrological symbolism

From the passage from Porphyry we learn, amongst other things, that the mithraic cosmos was endowed with a symbolic structure of an astrological character[10]. This structure, made up of subdivisions, alludes to the stages of a journey that correspond to the journey made by the soul into the world beyond.

Mithraeum of S. Clemente: the so-called "mithraic school". A meeting room for the faithful where it is likely that the adepts received instruction before being admitted to the more intimate secrets of the triclinium. On the walls there are seven niches, covered with graffiti, now faded, referring to the seven degrees of initiation.

Celsus argued that the mysteries of Mithras taught the symbolic interrelationship between the two celestial revolutions – that of the fixed stars and that of the planets – and the "circular journey of the soul through them"[11]. The idea of the soul's journey through the cosmos was common to many religions that had been influenced by neo-Platonism. Apuleius writes: "I reached the frontier of death, placed my foot on the threshold of Proserpine's realm; on my return I was transported through all the elements of the cosmos"[12]. In Mithraism it took on a particularly important role, directing the decision of the devotee (*miste*) to pursue an inner path to redemption. This journey had to be accomplished in stages by means of a progressive initiation which was focused around seven grades[13]. The first was the Raven (*Corax*); the second, the Occult (*Cryphius* or *Nymphus*, Nymph[14]); the third, the Soldier (*Miles*[15]); the fourth, the Lion (*Leo*); the fifth, the Persian (*Perses*); the sixth, the Runner of the Sun (*Heliodromus*; the seventh, the Father (*Pater*). This individual quest for purification symbolized in turn that of the soul. Associated with the seven grades were the seven doors, the seven planetary spheres, the seven days of the week, and the seven metals. The Moon (silver) was assigned to the first door, Mercury (iron) to the second, Venus (tin) to the third, the Sun (gold) to the fourth, Mars (alloy) to the fifth, Jupiter (bronze) to the sixth, and Saturn (lead) to the seventh. In addition to this, the signs of the zodiac were associated with the planets[16] in a complex series of connections.

In carrying out its journey into the upper heavens, the soul had to pass through seven celestial spheres (the seven planets) thereby freeing itself from the astral influences associated with each of the planets crossed, influences aquired originally when the soul had passed in the other direction, down towards earth. As it passed across the Moon, the soul was thought to cast off its vital and nutritive energy; on Mercury its desires; on Venus, its erotic inclinations; on the Sun, its intellectual capacities; on Mars, its warlike ardor; on Jupiter, its ambitions; and, finally, on Saturn, *accidia*, or sloth. This purificatory journey, involving the shedding of the passions, was symbolically enacted by the initiate as he went through the progressive stages of the initiation rites[17].

Facing: triclinium of the mithraeum of S. Clemente. The side benches are clearly seen, together with the central altar with the carved image of Mithras killing the bull, and the vault with its 11 openings of which four represent the seasons and the remainder the seven constellations.

Below: mithraeum of the Circus Maximus. Marble relief with the tauroctonia.

Nothing is known of the trials that the initiates had to overcome, apart from vague allusions which seem to suggest that the neophyte had to jump blindfolded across a ditch, his hands bound by chicken's entrails, or be witness to simulated murder. Whatever the case, the trials were designed to demonstrate control over the realm of feelings and emotions, which would lead to a kind of self-control similar in many ways to the "apathy" of the Stoics.

During the ceremony, the initiates wore animal masks, corresponding to the grade to which they belonged. If, for example, they were of the Lion grade, they would behave like a lion. This imitative behavior thus found its rationale in a form of visual identification of the animal with the deity. Indeed the central act of the Mithraic religion was an animal sacrifice, albeit one dignified by a cosmic and universal salvation.

The rituals

The admission ceremony for a new candidate had a hieratic character of great solemnity. Tertullian writes: "When one of these is initiated in a cave [...], he is offered a crown on the end of a sword: the ritual consists of a kind of counterfeiting of martyrdom. After the crown has been set firmly on his head, he is invited to remove it, with a gesture of refusal, and finally to put it back on the sword, declaring that Mithras alone is his crown.

From that day onwards he will no longer wear any crown on his head, an act of symbolic value indicating that, should he ever find himself put to the test about his oath of loyalty to the army, he will immediately be believed to be a soldier of Mithras, as he has thrown away the crown and declared that it is within his god"[18].

In the blackness of the Mithraic caves, feebly lit by flickering torches and candles, the initiated celebrated their ritual in honor of the god Mithras. Songs and hymns were sung to him in a state of drunkenness, exultation and abandon not unlike that of shamans, aided by the drinking of *haoma*. "Oh golden Haoma, I ask of you wisdom, might and victory, health and healing, prosperity and greatness, strength of body and knowledge of all things. May I go through the world as absolute master, crushing evil"[19]. The worshippers were required to perform purifying ablutions similar to the Christian baptism. The form of the ritual, though not known, is thought to have been linked to the different stages of initiation.

A banquet formed part of the ceremony, in which the mithraic *agape* was eaten with bread and wine. The obvious analogy with the Eucharist alarmed the Christians, who warned against the dangers of a demonic counterfeit. "In imitation, the evil demons have laid it down that the same [as the Eucharist] shall be done in the mysteries of Mithras: for the bread and a cup of water are presented with certain words that you know or can learn"[20]. Unfortunately, the

formulae used are not known, although some scholars believe they are preserved in a papyrus in the Bibliothèque Nationale in Paris[21]. The choice of a banquet as a central ritual act in the Mithraic liturgy sanctioned the act of the final sacrifice of the bull[22] through the eating of bread, the product of the bull's blood and spine. In the myth, when the young god plunges his blade into the belly of the ferocious beast, a vine springs from its blood, while miraculous ears of wheat grow from its tail. This is clearly a theological sublimation of some archaic agrarian sacrifice in which the annual sacrifice of a bull was thought to ensure the growth of new vegetation and, particularly, of corn. This vision of fertility was augmented by another, eschatological myth which was connected with the beginning and end of the world.

Tauroctonia

One sacred image, carved or painted, occupied a central place in the mithraic cave. It was an icon rich with significance, intended to sum up in a single image the entire religious and symbolic paradigm of

Barberini Mithraim. Detail of one of the scenes (first in the bottom row on the right-hand side) that surround the central depiction with the tauroctonia. Here, Mithras is seen with his red cloak, offering a piece of meat to a kneeling figure. It is a scene of investiture, or perhaps an oath of allegiance between Mithras and the Sun.

DEO·SOLI·INVIC

Mithraism. It depicts a young god with golden hair, barely restrained beneath a Phrygian cap, and a broad billowing cloak. He is plunging a long knife into the belly of a muscular and recalcitrant bull. A dog and a snake are licking its blood and a scorpion, reaching up towards the animal's testicles, attempts to catch its seed. This is the culminating moment of the myth: *tauroctonia*, the killing of the bull. For the initiates of the mithraic Mysteries, the victory over the wild bull was the affirmation of order over primordial barbarism, and its inevitable evolution towards the civilizing of mankind. Not all the initiates were capable of understanding the more subtle implications, or the more advanced cosmological and astrological speculations. Only a small elite, belonging to the upper levels of initiation, could grasp the more complicated examples that endowed Mithras with demiurgic powers. By killing the primordial bull, Mithras was creating the universe. From this action sprang the movement of the planets which, with their rotation around the heavens, gave life to Time.

The inevitability of Time

The idea of Time as an entity without limits (Zurvan Akarana) was already present in ideas associated with the followers of Mazda. In Mithraism it took on a central role. Astrologers saw in the actions of the planets and signs the fatal

and inexorable determination of the course of the universe. Time, as expressed through the causal action of the planetary influences, thus took on a quality of inevitability, representing the tragic aspect of Mithraic views, which were shared by other contemporary fatalistic trends such as Stoicism.

In many mithraea the statue of a lion-headed monster has been found (Zurvan, Kronos, Saturn), a symbolic representation of the qualities of Time, with its potential to devour, and its speed in running. It is a terrifying image: both man and beast, with wings, the head of a lion, and a body wound round with the coils of

Mithraeum of the Circus Maximus. Details of the marble relief. To the left, the Sun with the radiant crown. This planet takes on a pre-eminent role in the mithraen religion, as in the mythical events. The dog and the serpent (above) are the other components of the animal theophany of Mithraism. The first stood for the powers of God. The second, together with the scorpion, represented the opposite, being animals sent by Ahriman (the god of Evil) to oppose the good effects of the sacrifice of the bull.

a snake. The wings indicate the speed of Time; the lion's head with gaping jaws, Time's voracity. The coils of the snake's body, on the other hand, symbolize the cyclical movements of the stars and the heavenly bodies that govern the flow of Time. "The movement of the sun, while never departing from an elliptical path, pushes towards the upper and the lower ends of its cycle with variations determined by the alternating direction of the winds, tracing a course that resembles the coils of a snake"[23]. The monster bears the signs of the zodiac and sometimes those of the seasons on the snake-like part of its body, or elsewhere. It also holds a scepter and thunderbolt, indicating its status as a sovereign god[24]. It is often depicted holding one or two keys, a reference to the sun which, in its daily journey, opens the gates to the sky; to the east when it rises and to the west when it sinks. Thus Time is the maker and destroyer all things, the lord and leader of the four elements of the cosmos, in whom the power of all the gods is contained.

The triple Mithras

Along with the terrible figure of the leon-tocephalous *Kronos*, the sanctuary would also have contained statues or bas-reliefs of two youths, exactly resembling the Persian god, with cloaks and Phrygian caps. These were known as *Cautes* and *Cautopates*, or sometimes the *dadophori* (or torch-bearers)[25], and were often repre-

sented alongside Mithras, and stand on either side of him in the *tauroctonia*. One holds his torch aloft, the other points it downwards; with Mithras they form a triad, the "triple Mithras". These figures are visual embodiments of the god referring, by their arrangement, to the sun's heavens: dawn (*Cautes* – raised torch), noon (Mithras) and sunset (*Cautopates* – inverted torch). In addition, they represent the two extremities of existence: the heat of life and the freezing chill of death.

This introduction allows us to enter the mithraic caves with an understanding of Mithraism, and to interpret the many symbols and icons that are displayed in these ancient sanctuaries. To venture into these underground recesses is an unforgettable experience when backed up by an informed historical perspective, allowing us to see in the walls now rough and eroded by time the echoes of an arcane and mysterious cult, whose initiation rites are not so different from the liturgies of present-day esoteric sects.

Not many mithraic caves have survived in the west, except in Rome[26]. Of the many that remain there, only a few are accessible and then often only with special permission. They are a fascinating legacy whose rough and hypogeum-like appearance only adds to their attraction. As we have seen, the mithraic *specus* was created underground for particular religious reasons. Often created at different depths below ground, the most accessible of these sites are only reached by runged ladders, many of ancient origin.

The choice of a dark, underground place was, as we have seen, deliberately symbolic, and part of the exclusive and elitist nature of the religion. In almost all cases the sites were artificially created, made to resemble caves with special additions such as the use of pumice. They are generally rectangular in plan – the main hall at least – with long benches running down either side. Here the faithful sat to eat the mithraic *agape*. Other more functional rooms lead off the main one (vestibule, *schola*, *apparitorium*). These were often adapted for other uses later.

We can imagine the worshippers as they penetrated into the obscurity of these caves, scarcely illuminated by the few flickering torches. The few flames to pierce the darkness would probably have lit up those images of the greatest religious significance, making the sanctuary more awe-inspiring to the worshipper, and focusing on the central icon of the *tauroctonia*, the disturbing image of the leontocephalous monster, and the statues of the dadophori. We can imagine their chants and hymns; the figure of a man in the Raven's mask spinning crazily and cawing loudly under the inebriating effect of *haoma*[27]; the *Pater*, shaking the *tintinnabulum* (a kind of bell) as he reveals the sacred icon of the bull-slaying god, and then guarding the sacred flame.

These damp and humid caves are filled with the echoes of a buried liturgy. Amid the strong smell of *haoma* and incense, a throng of masked figures consume bread

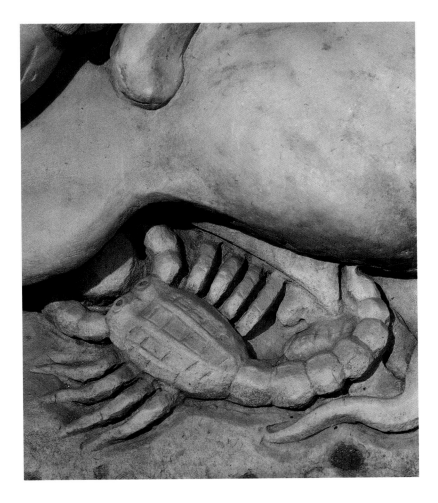

and wine. Suddenly the torches are extinguished and the stench of blood is overpowering. A bull has been sacrificed to a Persian god for the salvation of the cosmos and of mankind. Its lifeblood flows through the grating, bathing the worshipper in a warm baptismal liquid: the initiation ceremony of *taurobolium*.

The chanting ceases, and the feverish activity of a few moments earlier gives way to an absolute silence that unites the thoughts of a circle of figures as they meditate on their destiny, in search of a spark of immortality.

Mithraeum of the Circus Maximus. Detail of the marble relief with the scene of the tauroctonia. *In the foreground, the scorpion, symbol of the powers of Evil.*

The Mithraeum of the Circus Maximus

Not far from the Bocca della Verita, beneath what was once the Panatella pasta factory (today used by the Teatro dell'Opera as a costume store), the strange atmosphere of these ancient initiation rites can be experienced.

At varying depths below the storerooms is a mithraeum, a subterranean sanctuary built within a vast public building of the second century AD, facing

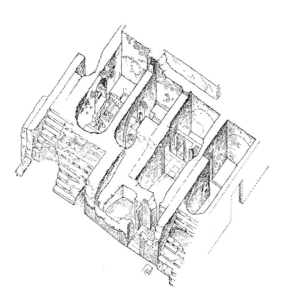

the *carceres*[1] of the Circus Maximus. In this building, the use of which is not clear, a group of believers loyal to the old Indian-Persian religion met in the third century AD. As always, their sanctuary was created in an underground site.

The mithraic *spelaeum* is reached by descending a long ladder. An intense and oppressive darkness defines its boundaries and signals that the visitor is passing into "another" dimension. The descent itself is a sort of initiation into the ancient cult, marking a journey into the distant past.

The first thing we notice, on the right, is a small room with a marble-clad niche. From its position and form, it would be reasonable to interpret this as an *apparitorium*, or sacristy. Crossing the hall, we discover two blind niches, one before the other. What were these niches intended for? Their presence at the entrance to the Mithraeum gives no room for doubt: here were certainly placed the statues of the victorious Mithras' inseparable

Inscriptions found in the mithraic cave and now displayed in the atrium that leads up to the archway covering the cult niche.

*Plan of the mithraeum.
The following rooms are
clearly visible: vestibule,*
apparitorium, *double-
halled triclinium.*

companions: *Cautes* and *Cautopates*, or the triple Mithras.

In the next room can be seen the usual *podia*, the benches where the worshippers sat during the ceremony of the sacred banquet, the mithraic *agape*. The bench was a useful shelf for the food, drink and lanterns.

In the next space are two more niches, the right-hand one containing a clay vessel, possibly intended for the cleansing water needed for baptism.

Covered with painted plaster, these two niches were originally graced with aedicules, adding a suitably monumental appearance to an underground place of worship. Below a large archway opening on to the main entrance to the sanctuary – the true *sancta sanctorum* of the Mithraeum – a large circle of alabaster

relieves the uniform pavement of reused marble, a gleaming contrast to the differently veined materials – gray marble, *cipollino*, and coral-colored *breccia*.

Further on, there is a circular opening, little more than half a meter deep, that once held an amphora containing some bones and two pig's teeth. It is clear that this cavity, originally fitted with a marble cover, had a religious function.

Opposite stands an object of rare beauty which is the major attraction of this Mithraeum: a large marble relief with the usual image of the *tauroctonia*, or killing of the bull. This was the sacred icon and so the most venerated image in the mithraic sanctuaries, in which the mythical deed of Mithras killing the bull is portrayed. The Sun and the Moon look on, seeming to participate in the event,

Right: the large relief with the scene of the tauroctonia. *This work of high quality dating from the third century AD was found lying on the floor of the cave and was probably the icon of the cult. An inscription with the name of the donor can be seen above.*

Below: bases for statues and cult images flanking the main niche.

the Sun turning his eyes to Mithras, whose cloak is being held up in the beak of the Raven. *Cautes* and *Cautopates,* with their torches, are witnesses to the event. Unlike other representations of the *tauroctonia,* this version is characterized by the appearance on the left-hand side of the scene of the so-called *transitus.* This shows the moment when Mithras, having captured the bull, leads it into the cave. Why is it that the donor of this relief should wish to emphasize this particular incident?

From the inscription above the border we learn the name of the donor: Tiberius Claudius Hermes[2]. Possibly he chose the subject. We know that the *transitus* had a specific symbolic meaning celebrating the trials of the initiate's journey. It is possible that Tiberius Claudius Hermes wished his gift to convey the difficulties

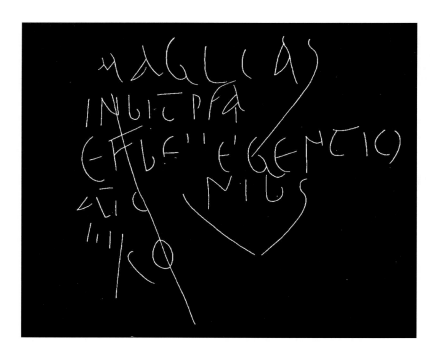

Above: this ancient graffito is on the back wall of the triclinium (high up on the left). Its meaning has not yet been fully interpreted.

Facing: the large arch at the back of the triclinium. This was the most sacred part of the mithraic cave and, with its collection of statues and images, the place to which the eyes of the devotees were drawn.

been a statuette of the god that would have drawn the ecstatic eyes of the worshippers at the culminating moment of the liturgy.

High up, to the left of the arch, next to two brackets that must once have supported a lintel, there is an almost illegible trace of graffiti. The message is hard to understand and has not been fully interpreted, but it leaves no doubt about the value placed on the magic arts. The *magicas*[7] scratched on the wall of this mithraic cave speaks of the close links still felt between this group of initiates[8] and the Magi of Persia; or rather, with the Magusai who took and transformed the Zoroastrian Mithras – with the addition of astrology, astralism and the magic arts studied by the Chaldaeans and Babylonians – into the character of the Roman Mithras.

On the right-hand side is another small relief with the usual representation of the *tauroctonia*. This is another element in the original decorative scheme which defines the wealth and fascination of this mithraic sanctuary that has stood since time immemorial within the heart of the store rooms of the Teatro dell'Opera.

of initiation as well. It is a work of good quality[3], its size and position (when discovered it was lying on the ground) suggesting it was probably the cult icon, worshipped in the niche on the back wall before this was altered.

A large arch, its inner surface clad in pumice[4], divides the main space of the mithraic triclinium and marks the site of the densest concentration of idols. A series of bases of varying shapes and of uncertain use surround this sacred treasury, hinting at the richness of the decoration, now unfortunately lost. While it is reasonable to suppose that the two bases on either side of the arch were for statues of the Sun and the Moon, it is not so easy to guess what was supported by the others[5], particularly those with triangular tops.

Inside a niche, formerly covered in splendid marble[6], there must once have

The Barberini Mithraeum

Concealed among the shady walks of the gardens of this Baroque palace is a Mithreaum, whispering the mysteries of an ancient initiatory sect.

Just past the palace a broad ramp leads up to Villa Savorgnan di Brazzà[1] (1936) that jealously guards within its walls the ancient *spelaeum*. A stair leads down to a cave that is notable as one of the few mithraic sites to have preserved its painted decoration. The main icon illustrates scenes from the life of Mithras.

The building is a small subterranean edifice, showing a number of different periods of construction[2]. Rectangular in plan, with a barrel vault and lateral benches, as was common with this type of building, it occupies one of three sites found during work on the villa. The low vault presses onto the room, accentuating the gloominess of the space and the dark roughness of the walls, still partly covered in plaster. Painted on one of the pillars is a female figure, which can be interpreted as being in an attitude of offering. The benches for the worshippers tilt towards the walls and have the usual indentations. An inscription on the bench on the right gives the name of the donor: "Iperante has offered this base as a gift to the invincible god Mithras"[3].

In the center, an altar, pierced to allow smoke to escape, reminds us of the duty of the *Pater* – the highest stage of intiaitate and priest – to guard the perpetual flame. He would offer a prayer to the Sun three times a day: at dawn, at midday and at dusk, turning towards each compass point in turn. It was he who sacrificed the beasts, gathering their blood in a ditch, and who presided over libations and the official rituals of the cult.

Dominating the scene is the great fresco on the back wall. The figure of the god, slaying the bull, stands out from a light background, accompanied by the visible symbolic figures of the inseparable dadophori. To this extent, the depiction repeats the standard iconography, but, looking at the upper section, we see a

number of interesting elements that distinguish this version from others; a broad semi-circular band bears the symbols of the zodiac with the figure of Kronos in the center. The leontocephalous monster appears, as ruler of the cosmos and of the planetary influences, who, wrapped in the elliptical coils of the snake, holds sway over the sphere of the Universe. Above, the Sun and the Moon, in facing half-busts, observe this moving procession of signs as though participating in the movement of the cosmos of which Mithras is the demiurge. Pisces, Aquarius, Capricorn, Sagittarius, Scorpio and Libra are shown on one side; Virgo, Leo, Cancer, Gemini, Taurus and Aries on the other, marking the zodiacal band which stresses the fatalistic and astrological character of the mithraic religion.

Mithras' cloak is decorated with stars[4] (there are seven, that being the number of fixed stars). By killing the cosmic bull, Mithras has created the universe, while

Left: fresco depicting the story of Mithras.

Below: plan of the mithraic triclinium.

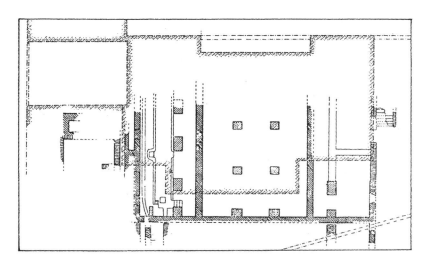

Detail of one of the scenes (second from the bottom, right-hand side) surrounding the central depiction of the tauroctonia. Mithras is shown standing and touching a semicircular line (the vault of heaven), his legs straddled between two little trees.

from the movement of his cloak comes the rotation of the fixed stars. The planets begin to move in the opposite direction, tracing a route marked by the signs of the zodiac. Thus from Mithras' sacrificial act Time is born, and its rhythm marked by the rotation of the celestial bodies. On either side of the central scene are ten smaller ones, arranged in two vertical strips of five, showing the mythical deeds of the god. The left side is now almost indecipherable, but the sequence can be reconstructed by looking at comparable arrangements, and also because when the whole fresco was discovered it was in a considerably better state. The first scene shows Jupiter hurling a thunderbolt at a gigantic snake-tailed monster, recalling

the episode of the struggle between Jupiter and the giants[5]. The second scene shows a recumbent female figure that can perhaps be interpreted as the *Terra Mater*, impregnated by the waters of *Coelus* to give life to *Oceanus*[6]. The third shows Mithras being born from a rock and brandishing a knife and a torch, accompanied by the dadophori: this is one of the most common representations of the birth of Mithras. The fourth scene depicts Mithras shooting an arrow to strike the rock near to which a worshipper waits to quench his thirst. The story, with its close paralells to that of Moses, forms part of a series of stories relating to the birth of the first human couple, and the trials that this couple has to undergo in the face of the opposition of the god of Evil, Ahriman. The fifth and last of the scenes on the left shows the episode of the *transitus*, with Mithras leading the bull into the cave. On the right-hand side, starting from the bottom, we see the standing Mithras offering a piece of meat (or a drinking horn) to a kneeling figure. This scene may represent the pact of homage between Mithras and the Sun. The following scene shows Mithras standing with legs supported by two trees, touching a semicircular line (the vault of heaven). This scene is a visual interpretation of the notion that Mithras, as god of light, is also the *mesites* or "inhabitant of the middle zone"; insofar as light, brought by the air, is an intermediary between heaven and earth[7]. The third scene shows Mithras and

another figure (almost certainly the Sun) holding up two spears before an altar, thus sealing the pact of alliance between Mithras and the Sun. The fourth episode gives a glimpse of the Sun standing in his chariot and inviting Mithras to take his place beside him. The last scene concludes the series with a depiction of the sacred banquet in which Mithras and six companions, reclining on a couch that is scattered with cushions, carry out the central act of the rite, the conclusion of the mythical sacrifice[8].

Inscription from the right-hand bench. The name of the donor is clearly legible: "Iperans has offered this bench to the undefeated god Mithras."

The Mithraeum of S. Clemente

The most famous of all the subterranean sites, S. Clemente is not only easy to get into, but also offers a very interesting and complex layout. Inside, it is possible to identify four different levels, all very different in character and structure.

The credit for the discovery of this lower church is due to Father Mullooly, a former prior of this church, and the great archaeologist De Rossi. Together, in 1857, these two men carried out preliminary excavations, uncovering, as well as the lower basilica dating from the fourth century AD, a lower level with remains from the first century AD. For a long time it was not possible to investigate this third archaeological stratum any further, due to a water course[1] which had found a way in through the walls and submerged the area in question.

It was not until 1912 that permission was obtained to drain the flooded area, a courageous intervention from Father Nolan. This was done by means of a conduit, approximately 700 m. long, that led from S. Clemente to the Cloaca Maxima, behind the Colosseum. This time, a fourth level came to light, comprising a number of houses destroyed by the fire of 64 AD during Nero's reign. These buildings had been filled with earth and used as the foundations of new buildings (on the third level), which can be seen today on either side of a passageway.

It was on the lowest level that a Mithraeum was discovered, made up of a series of rooms created in the second half of the second century, within the walls of an older *domus* (perhaps publicly owned, and dating from the end of the first century). Distinguishable among these rooms is the so-called Mithraic School: this was a rectangular space where it seems probable that adepts were given instruction before being admitted to the more intimate secrets of the triclinium or banqueting hall. They would certainly have been of the lower initiatory grades – *Corax, Cryphius (Nymphus)* and *Miles* –

who were forbidden to participate in the mithraic *agape*. The room must have been finely decorated, with a mosaic pavement of black and white tesserae, and some stucco work now in a poor state of repair. Seven niches are set into the walls, covered with graffiti that, although now very faint, related to the seven grades of initiation. It is not difficult to imagine the symbolic instruction of the worshippers that took place in a room like this; the stern and difficult catechism; the initiations based on the overcoming of trials in which the adept progressively advanced towards a kind of internal catharsis in order to achieve self-control in the sphere of the feelings and the emotions.

A hall (or vestibule) contains remains suggesting that this could be the anti-chamber where the *adepti* would have gathered together on the benches around the sides of the room, beneath a beautiful ceiling decorated with delicate geometric and floral designs.

The central part of the rite was performed in the triclinium. This was a long, narrow and gloomy room, made oppressive by a low vault clad in pumice. It was decorated with stucco stars and eleven openings, four representing the seasons and the remainder the seven constellations. The mithraic cave-cosmos was thus perfectly represented. It is possible that there was a desire to emphasize the starry vault, with its weighty symbolism, to the point of making it appear to spin round the heads of the faithful. "On the other hand, the cosmos was formed spontaneously and is of the same nature as matter, that the ancients referred to enigmatically as stone and rock because it appears to be inert and hostile to form, and they considered it to be infinite because of its amorphous being"[2]. This makes the relationship with the cave clear enough, but it also clarifies the allegory of the birth of Mithras represented in this hall by a small statue placed in a cavity of the *specus*, in line with the altar placed in the center of the sanctuary. The young god is shown here emerging upright from the rock, like the light from the solid vault of the sky. In the ancient Indian verses, his birth is described with the words: "leapt from the rock, came out of the cave."

S. Clemente. View of the lower church, showing the main nave and the piers supporting the upper storey. The remains of the pavement of the original Early Christian church can be seen in the foreground.

Running along the two long sides of the room are benches. Here the adepts would have reclined while participating in the ritual ceremony. On either side there are semicircular niches for statues, while at the far end is a small cavity that seems to have been used as a store, or as a place where the bones of sacrificed animals were placed.

It is the central altar, however, that provides the main decorative effect of this room. Made of luminous marble, it emerges from the dark shadows of the cave. The *tauroctonia* is portrayed on the front in a rather shallow relief; the overall treatment of the theme does not reveal any iconographic peculiarities, including as it does all the usual elements: Mithras, the bull, the dog, the scorpion, and the snake. And those inseparable compan- ions of Mithras, *Cautes* and *Cautopates*, stand on either side of the "invincible one" in the act of killing the bull; the Sun in the ascendant and the Sun declining, *mors et vita*. The dadophori, together with Mithras, represent the three-fold emblem of the divinity and extend his symbolic essence.

The Mithraeum of the Baths of Caracalla

Beneath the magnificent halls of the Baths of Caracalla lies a labyrinth of passageways and rooms, a network of galleries, *cryptae* and streets wide enough to take vehicles transporting provisions and laundry, firewood and all the other things needed to ensure the smooth operation of the baths. This lower world,

given over to the labors of slaves and servants, also provided a home for the cult of the Mysteries of the god Mithras, sometime around the third century AD.

A series of rooms have been found which correspond to the great north-west exedra above. This impressive complex includes a vestibule, latrines, and an *apparitorium* or changing room. The underground area is reached through a side gate. The first room, with a barrel vault, contains nothing of interest apart from a small semicircular basin, which is of uncertain function. This room leads into a space that was probably the vestibule, although the ceiling vault has now collapsed.

Moving on, we cross a marble threshold into a large room with four groin vaults opening out, illuminated by a vast aperture of light opening at the back. This is a *spelaeum*, perhaps the largest in the city, soundly constructed behind the gloomy rows of pillars. As usual, the two long side benches[1], narrowing slightly

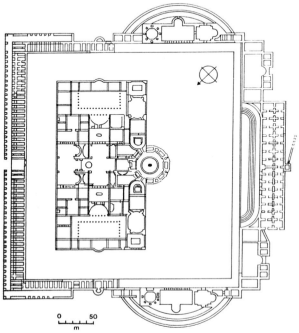

0   50
m

Fresco in the niche on the right-hand wall of the triclinium.

remains of a fresco where we can still make out a male figure with a Phrygian cap, clearly Mithras or one of his companions *Cautes* or *Cautopates*.

A vast mosaic with black and white geometric designs covers the floor space. The pattern is interrupted by a large clay bowl, sunk into the ground and closed with a marble ring, where it is likely that the purificatory ablutions forming part of the ritual were performed. This ceremony was declared a demonic imitation of baptism by the Church Fathers, and particularly by Tertullian, who had no hesitation in declaring that "even those without the slightest intellectual understanding of the divine powers believe that their idols can perform the same wonders through baptism, but they deceive themselves with mere water"[3].

Another large opening breaks the surface of the pavement, and represents the major interest of this mithraeum. It is a large, deep hole linked to a passageway that comes out into neighboring rooms which were used as an *apparitorium* (changing room). This may have been one of the many arrangements for the transport of the sacrificed bull, or a way of emphasizing the theatrical elements of the initiatory trials, almost like a stage set, but we cannot be certain. What is clear is that access from the service rooms, joining directly and beneath the ground with the ditch in the main room, is somewhat suggestive of the disturbing rituals of the *taurobolium*: the gory ablutions using the bull's blood that seem to characterize this

towards the upper end, indicate the banqueting function of the sanctuary. A long shelf, intended for lanterns, torches and other objects necessary to the mithraic ritual, follows the line of the room. The two benches are not attached to the walls, as is common, but have passageways down the inner sides, almost like aisles[2]. Four very small niches carved out of the benches probably had a similar function to those found at S. Clemente. In the north-west wall, near the corner, a rectangular niche contains the faint

and other oriental cults. Indeed it seems that, for the ritual of the *Magna Mater*, believers submitted to a horrifying baptism of this sort, lowering themselves into the ditches – known as *fossae sanguinis* – in the belief that the hot blood of the bull pouring down on them would cleanse them of their impurities.

Before the ritual entered its central phase, there must have been a large number of other religious ceremonies, and for these other rooms were allocated, where the initiates dressed,

undressed, or kept their sacred objects. The *apparitorium*, with a low bench along the back wall supported by four small arches, was certainly conceived for this purpose and designed to connect with the main hall via the underground passageway mentioned above.

Two small square rooms situated on either side of the passage were clearly used as latrines, given that one is placed over a drain and the other has a small waste hole, down which rubbish was obviously thrown.

Back wall of the triclinium, today opened up allowing in a dramatic but historically unlikely flood of daylight.

This is, then, a mithraic complex with all the anterooms necessary for the enactment of the cult rituals. This *spelaeum*, once richly decorated, must have made a dramatic effect. There is particular evidence for this in the discovery of a headless statue of Venus, found, along with many other sculptural remains, in the *spelunca magna* of the complex. How can we explain the presence of the goddess Venus here?

It is known that a number of inscriptions referring to the cult of Mithras mention Venus Genitrix. There are also bas-reliefs depicting the goddess of love and beauty, twisting up her hair and looking in a mirror, as in the sculpture of Praxiteles. It is hard to know where the statue stood, but it is thought that it may have been one of a group of statues decorating the apse at the end of the room, today illuminated by a spectacular but certainly not original opening. In reality it was a deep darkness and a damp, heavy atmosphere that would have greeted the worshipper stepping into this and other mithraic caves; the despised subterranean world of the *castra tenebrarum*.

The room used as a changing room. Some scholars think that it was a stable, in which case the structure on the back wall could be interpreted as a manger.

DEATH

The Manes and the cult of the dead

The Manes were the spirits of the dead, supernatural beings who could be propitiated or warded off by prayer and who, according to Roman tradition, roamed around the houses of married couples like ghostly members of the family. If proper homage was paid to them, they were capable of helping their descendants; if neglected they could be quite vindictive or vicious, taking on the more sinister form of *lemures* or *larvae*[1] who came to disturb the peace and the sleep of the living "[…] he says that death came to him in a dream"[2].

To ward off such fears, the Romans had recourse to special formulae and rituals, described in great detail by Ovid:

"At midnight when silence invites us to sleep,
and you fall silent, o dogs and multicolored birds,
he who remembers the ancient ritual and fears the gods
jumps from his bed without pausing to slip on his sandals
and snaps his fingers, using the middle finger with the thumb
so as not to meet any shadowy spirit, and stays silent.
After he has cleansed his hands in the fountain's waters,
he turns and first puts black beans in his mouth;
then he throws them over his shoulder, saying as he does so:
'I throw them, and thus save myself and my family from harm
with these beans!' Nine times he says it, nor does he turn to look
behind him. He believes that the spirit picks them up and follows
him unseen. Again he bathes, strikes the bells of Temesa,
and prays that the spirit will leave his house.
'Spirits of my ancestors, depart' he repeats nine times;
he turns and believes the ritual has been accomplished with purity."[3]

Preceding pages: the tomb of the Pancratii and one of the white stucco tondi from the tombs in the Via Latina.
Above: one of the four figures from the vault in the burial chamber of the Pyramid of Caius Cestius (eighteenth-century engraving).
Right: detail of the stucco ceiling of the Pancratii tomb.
Facing: interior of columbarium VII in the Ostiense necropolis.

This was an individual ritual designed to placate the lonely and hungry spirits, and to exorcise the fear of the presence of *lemuri* or of the malicious and dangerous *larvae*. The whole ritual was performed with great deference and care: the ritual cleansing in pure spring water, the use of the black beans, the striking of the bells. Behind the constant repetition of the formulae and the lively expressiveness of Ovid's narrative, it is possible to imagine the spirits as they emerge from the

shadows following the various rites as they are performed in turn.

The *Manes* were almost always invoked in inscriptions with the traditional formula *D(is) M(anibus)* or *D(is) M(anibus) S(acrum)*[4] followed by the name or names of the deceased, in the genitive or dative case.

The Romans' veneration of the dead formed part of a culture founded partly on their respect for the memory of their own dead relatives and partly on the supersti-

tious reasons referred to above. There were many public occasions connected with this culture, and a number of private ones, such as the *dies natalis* (anniversary of the deceased's birthday). Among the most important was the commemoration of the dead, such as the *Parentalia*[5] or *dies Parentales*, which lasted from 13 to 21 February. The last day of this period, *Feralia*, was intended for public rituals, while the preceding days were for private family ceremonies. All these occasions – *Feralia*, *Lemuria* or *Parentalia* – involved particular and devout attention to the mortal remains in their tombs and to the tending of them. This went from the simplest of food offerings – bread and grapes – to sweets and sausages, and even actual banquets with guests (*epulae*) sharing food with the deceased. No expense was spared: incense, fruit, flowers of every kind, particularly violets and roses, believed to ensure an eternal spring in the next life. "Sprinkle my ashes with wine and perfumed oil of lavender: / o guest, and add balsam to the red roses. / My unmourned urn enjoys a perpetual Spring. / I am not dead, I have only changed worlds"[6].

Funerary rites

Complex ritual preparations were required for a funeral (*funus*) and the period preceding the ceremony. The occasion varied, of course, according to the social and economic status of the person involved. The richer the deceased had been, the more important the public or military posts he had held, the more solemn and elaborate was the funeral: (*funus publicum*, *funus militare*, or even *funus imperatorum*).

Facing: columbaria in Vigna Codini. A good example of the neat arrangement of niches (right-hand wall), intended to contain the ashes of the deceased. The word columbarium *comes from* columba (dove) *because the walls of niches resemble those of a dovecote.*

Above: tombs in the Via Latina, the Pancratii burial place. Detail of the stucco ceiling showing mythological scenes. This one illustrates the episode of the Judgment of Paris. In the center is Mercury, encouraging Paris to choose which of the three goddesses is the most beautiful.

The task of organizing the rites fell to the *pater familias*, or to his successor if he himself had died. First, the dead person was kissed (since it was believed that the soul left the body by way of the mouth), then his name was pronounced loudly three times (*conclamatio*), in a last salute. Then specially selected *libitinarii* washed the body, annointing it with perfumed oils and other potions. Once robed again, the corpse was placed in the atrium of the house with its feet pointing towards the entrance. The exposure of the body continued for many days, which required that the hall be sprinkled with strongly scented essences (candles, boxes of incense, and flowers) in order to disguise the odor of decomposition. Indeed, a form of embalming was not infrequently employed in order to delay the unpleasant effects of decay. A coin was often placed in the mouth, the *obulus Carontis*, the ferryman's fee for carrying the dead person from Earth to Hades.

If the deceased was an adult male of rank, the impression of a likeness, or

Above: the Portland vase (end of the first century AD), in an eighteenth-century engraving, an exquisite glass-cameo now in the British Museum, London. It was for a time believed to have been part of the funerary goods from Monte del Grano.

Right: detail of the cover of the sarcophagus from Monte del Grano.

Facing: the vast circular chamber inside the mound of Monte del Grano.

death mask, was permitted, provided that it conformed to precise legal requirements (*ius imaginum*). The mask (*imago*), made of wax, precisely reproduced the lineaments of the face. "The image resembles the deceased very closely in appearance and coloring. On the occasion of public sacrifices, the Romans display these images and honor them with great solemnity. When someone else important in the family dies, the images participate in the funeral, being used to disguise people similar to the dead person in height and form. If the dead person had been a consul or military leader, they put on robes edged with scarlet, if a censor, purple togas, if he had been awarded a triumph or similar honor, garments embroidered with gold. Thus dressed, these figures were carried in wheeled vehicles, while before them were carried fasces and axes, and the other emblems associated with magistrates, according to the honors that the person had received from the state in his lifetime. When the procession reached the Rostra, all were seated in order on seats of ivory. It would be difficult for a young man loving honor and virtue to imagine a more beautiful spectacle. Who would not be stirred to emulate such virtue, on seeing gathered together the images of such outstanding men, as if still alive and breathing? What could be more beautiful than such a sight?"[7].

The *funus*, then, was often a grand ceremony using theatrical devices to strong emotive effect. The funeral

procession was headed by the corpse lying on a litter. This was followed by the close relatives dressed in black, and a group of women hired for the occasion whose theatrical mourning was a dramatic represention of the sorrow of the whole family. Sometimes they had receptacles attached below their eyes to catch their tears, thus providing evidence of the authenticity of their grief. The ceremony was accompanied by musicians, mimers and dancers who – in the case of someone illustrious – attended the procession all the way to the Forum, where the ceremony was concluded with the funeral oration on the Rostra.

The tombs

The attention given to the ritual and ceremony of the funeral helps our understanding of the origin and arrangement of tombs[8]. From the earliest type of burial with cremation to interment, from the simple *stele* to the more elaborate monumental forms of the mausoleum, Roman tombs emphasize an attachment to the reality of life, and the strong desire on the part of the living to overcome death through the preservation of the memory of the deceased. The view of the dead person as being in close contact with the living and with the members of his family and his *gens* was commonly held. The central idea can be summed up in the phrase: *non omnis morior* – I shall not be entirely dead. This ideal contact and

conversation between the dead and the living is apparent from the way burial areas were arranged, where the desire to be exposed to the eyes of the living led to the tombs being set up along the edges of main thoroughfares rather than in more densely inhabited areas within the city. The almost tangible presence of the deceased, with their portrait-mask, and inscription detailing minutely their deeds, reinforces this constant dialogue with the living. In some cases, the inscriptions even speak directly to the passer-by.

It is not easy to draw up a chronology for the architectural typology of these tombs. The choice of a funerary monument in Roman society, while sometimes following a particular fashion, was more often determined by the economic resources of the patron, or the social and political standing of the deceased. The type chosen was intended to express ideal values through its formal and decorative arrangement. In this chapter, we shall examine some of the more interesting examples of subterranean tombs and funeral monuments; *columbaria* will be discussed in a later chapter.

Left: tombs in the Via Latina: burial place of the Valerii. One of the white stucco tondi from the vault of the funerary chamber.

Following pages: three portrait busts of merchants in the columbaria of Vigna

The tombs on the Via Latina

On the south-eastern outskirts of the city, a fragment of the Roman Campagna, saved from the invading cement[1], still preserves intact its original appearance as an ancient road flanked by trees and tombs. Here, at the IV milestone of the Via

Latina, among the evergreens and tombs, one can rediscover a taste and enthusiasm for the past such as that experienced on a nineteenth-century *promenade*. The paved road leads out towards a quiet agrarian landscape, far from the roar of the traffic; its funerary *exempla* noble reminders of the past. The first landmark of architectural interest is the Barberini tomb. This elegant and dignified structure on several floors is made of a compact web of reddish bricks. Its lines are sober and composed, confining the description of the architectural elements to the two colors of the brickwork and recalling the *tempietti* popular in the Antonine period[2]. The upper story, once reached by an internal stair, must originally have been richly decorated, the vault covered with frescoes and painted stuccoes now blackened by repeated damage to the building, which was used as a shelter by farmers and shepherds.

Further along is the tomb of the Valeri[3]. The good condition of its exterior

is misleading, since it is not original and is in fact the product of a very free interpretation by nineteenth-century restorers. The underground approach, however, marked at its entrance by an atrium, amply makes up for any disappointment. The entrance reveals a dazzling array of white stuccoes, the half-formed shadows of the forms at first eclipsed by the tremendous impact of the whole. But gradually these rough and vague shapes begin to take on meaning. They become tritons, nereids, griffins and sea-monsters and create, without color and with great delicacy, a phantasmagoric underwater world. Dancing cupids and maenads weave a seemingly endless geometrical tapestry of roundels and quadrants across the ceiling.

One would search in vain for a key to the symbolism of the whole; what we find in the end is a lighthearted and sunny depiction of the next world, a sort of endless dance celebrating the journey into the Empyrean.

In the central medallion, a griffin carries the soul up into the heavens. The spiritual essence of the dead person takes on a feminine and tangible form, reconstructing the overall sense of this figurative tumult. Only then does the meaning becomes more apparent, translating a system of beatitude into a clear and ethereal apotheosis, where the geometric and harmonious rhythm is broken only by the allusive and temporal admonition of the Hours.

A further tomb concealing a surprising interior is that of the Pancrazi family. Here,

a large underground chamber, accessible by an original stairway, is preceded by a vestibule with a handsome brick bench running down the side, supported by little arches. A row of sarcophagi must have been arranged on this bench, which today is empty apart from one fluted example bearing the portrait of the deceased couple within a medallion[4].

Facing: stucco decoration with, in the center, a divine figure (possibly Ulysses). The delicate decorative motifs and the colors give the surfaces a playfully rhythmical and imaginative feel.

Below: in the foreground, two centaurs fighting with panthers.

The inner chamber is dominated by an enormous sarcophagus, the age and occupant of which is unknown[5]. The vault of the room is richly decorated in ochres, carmines and blues, in stucco and fresco. Griffins, candelabra, lions and centaurs, carved in the whitish plaster, frame the main episodes of the story. These depict Admetus, accompanied by Apollo and Diana, triumphantly pointing out to Pelias the cart with the harnessed beasts; Priam appearing before Achilles to claim the body of Hector; Paris choosing the most beautiful of the three goddesses; and, finally, Hercules received on Mount Olympus. All those in this crowd of gods and immortal heroes are marked out by the inevitable force of Fate, the supreme ruler, who watches over this world of stuccoes and paintings as over the actions of men.

Monte del Grano

The setting is a very ordinary square on the outskirts of the city, with deafening traffic and the standard, depressing arrangement of blocks of flats. The only unusual feature is a small rise topped with olive trees, adding a note of fresh greenery to an otherwise bland and monotonous concrete surrounding. The inhabitants of this district appear to be unaware of the ancient treasure in their midst, masking its presence behind a lively and colorful market. The Monte del Grano (Corn Hill) gives no hint of its man-made interior; even the name suggests a natural rather than a man-made form. According to local legend, the hill grew out of a large pile of wheat, gathered there on a feast day, which was destroyed as a punishment from the gods and turned into earth by a thunderbolt[1].

In fact, it is a magnificent tomb within a mound, or *tumulo*. Its shape in the form of an inverted cone resembles a *modius* (*modium grani*, or corn measure). This gives it, through a corruption of meaning,

its present name, as we learn from an ancient medieval document: "*et cum parte Modii sive Montanis vel Montis dello Grano.*"

The rich stepped decoration in travertine which covered the exterior has now completely disappeared. It was removed in 1387 by the owner of the site, Nicolò Valentini, in order to "*cavare extrahere et rumpere omnem quantitatem lapidum tiburtinarum existentium intus et extra montem qui vocatur Mons Grani*" and particularly to "*deducere et revertere in calcem bonam et congruam*"[2].

By the sixteenth century the monument, stripped of its marble exterior, had acquired a tower that, though restored by Lovatti in 1870, collapsed in 1900 during a hurricane. At the end of the nineteenth century, a magnificent sarcophagus dating from the third century AD[3] was discovered inside the mound, erroneously

Inside the image:

A

SCALA DI PALMI XL
5 10 15 20   40

thought to be that of Alexander Severus and his mother Mamea. "I remember, beyond Porta San Giovanni, a mile after the aqueducts, in the place called Monte del Grano, there was a great and ancient mound of rubble. It was easy work for someone to break into it and get inside, lowering himself down until he found a large sculptured tomb, showing the Rape of the Sabines. On the lid were two reclining figures with the features of Alexander Severus and Julia Mamea, his mother, while inside were found their ashes. This same tomb is now to be found on the Campidoglio, in the courtyard of the palazzo where the academies are"[4]. In fact, the sculpted narratives do not show scenes from the life of Alexander Severus and his mother Mamea, but scenes from the life of Achilles; but this explains why this tomb-mausoleum has at different times been attributed to the last of the

Cross-section of the mound, showing the entrance gallery, the circular chamber and the air vents (from an engraving by Piranesi).

Severus family. And the confusion does not end here. Some scholars have maintained that this sarcophagus concealed one of the most outstanding examples of glass-cameo work still in existence: the famous Portland Vase, dating from the end of the first century AD)[5], deservedly famous for its celebrated figurative decoration executed with great skill on the glass base. It is an exceptional piece whose quality reminds us of the refined taste of the patrons of that period, and of the pleasure they took in surrounding themselves with rare and precious objects[6].

A small gate concealed in the surrounding garden opens into the interior of the ancient mound, with a long *dromos* leading to a great round chamber. A thick covering of earth weighs down heavily on the building, now rough and neglected. The intense darkness and the heavy, damp atmosphere make it difficult to imagine the original impact of the whole, with its beautiful ring of marble columns. To reconstruct or imagine it as it was, we must refer to Piranesi's highly imaginative engraving, in which a simple mound of land outside the city is recreated as a major monument.

The Necropolises on the Via Ostiense

Facing: wall on the first floor, showing the many niches of the columbarium of the gens Pontia *(first century* AD*).*

Below: plan of the funerary complex. The area is a mass of tightly packed tombs, graves and loculi.

Not far from the basilica of S. Paolo fuori le Mura, a group of tombs and columbaria, huddled together under a single sheltering roof, chart the history of funerary customs from the early years of the Republic to the last days of the Empire[1]. Behind the fencing is a jumble of

loculi, little niches, sarcophagi, and chests resembling a storehouse from Hades. A rough path winds between the bones and ashes of both slaves and free men who sought to dispatch their last message to the living from these graves, in an everlasting *memento mori*. Here they present

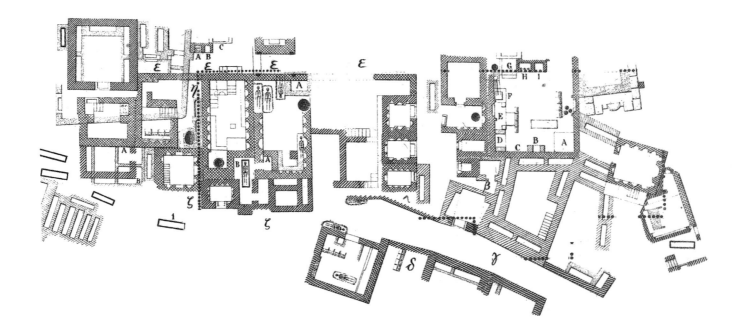

The distribution of the
funerary structures is
chronologically arranged
and diversified. Niches,
stelae and columbaria
follow one another
without apparent order in
an intricate and
labyrinthine sequence.

their family name, their ages and professions, with invocations to the Manes to protect them after death. The tombs, facing on to small roads and streets, present a certain architectural dignity not without touches of refinement. Whether the tombs are for an individual or a guild, they proudly display their inscriptions and sometimes evoke, in the delicate composition of the painted sections, the delights to come in the afterlife.

In the northern section of the necropolises, the oldest tombs are sober, with tufa facades, while those from the imperial period are made of brick. In the small area below the stairway to the side we find a peacock, while nearby, a muscular Hercules snatches Theseus from the jaws

The sequence of tombs and cinerary urns offers a broad range of types going from the early years of the Republic to the late Empire.

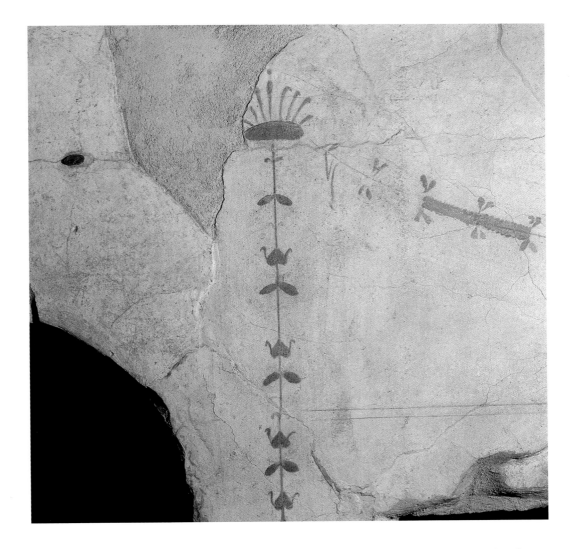

of Hades. This scene is found in a small painted recess, hidden among the tombs in the shadow of a stairway. The obscurity of its setting does not stop the image from throwing out its cry of defiance to death.

Not far away is a sizable burial area in *opus reticulatum*, roughly square, dating from the beginning of the Empire. Tombs from various periods are placed against the enclosing wall, in order to make the best use of the limited space available. Two niche tombs, one in marble and the other in brick, do not quite make up for the poverty of those around them, simple earth graves that are little more than ditches.

On the other side are two rectangular areas with walls pierced by niches that proclaim their use as columbaria. The first, closest to the entrance, has an elegant aedicule containing a depiction of two lionesses attacking a gazelle, framed by garlands of daisies. Next to this, an opening reveals the presence of a small

Facing: one of the frescoes of the columbaria facing onto a lane off the Via Ostiense.

Below: detail of the decoration.

well. The funerary vessels and inscriptions found here belong to the *gens Pontia* (first century AD).

Facing this, on a lane coming out onto the Via Ostiense, are other interesting columbaria (first century AD), arranged in sequence, lining up the brick-clad facades that were originally crowned by a triangular tympanum. One stands out in particular: that of Livia Nebris, daughter of Marcus, buried here with other members of her family. Floral motifs and delicate festoons cover the walls pierced with niches, enlivening the interior with an air of festivity. The travertine jamb provides us with the measurements, given with pedantic exactitude: *in fr(onte) p(edes) VI* (width), and *in ag(ro) p(edes) VIII* (length). All around the interior, facing one another, delicate figures appear to float among the plant motifs. To one side is an irregularly shaped room edged round with floor graves, which has been described as the seat of the college or family (*schola*) who provided these tombs for its members. Today is it difficult to make out the subject of the series of painted scenes with their flying figures. They seem generally to be birds that soar in the whiteness of the background, as if among the stars. Among griffins and winged horses, only the eagle on the globe seems to be at rest among the restless movement of imaginary figures.

The Mausoleum of Romulus

Above: fresco on the back wall of the vestibule, which shows a quadriga of a type dating from a later date.

Right: a find that documents the later use of this complex in Christian times.

Facing: interior of the vast cylindrical subterranean drum of the mausoleum with its enormous central pier.

Facing the *carceres* of the Circus of Maxentius, the tomb of Romulus is a revival of the sumptuous imperial dwellings of late antiquity. It is partly concealed by a large farmhouse, however, making it difficult to understand the original layout.

It was part of a residential complex[1] intended to celebrate the greatness of the emperor and of his *gens*, modeled on the new encomiastic parameters imported from the East, in which the villa, circus and mausoleum together served the needs of the political and architectural ideology of the fourth century. The complex celebrated the quasi-divine role of the emperor who was acclaimed in the circus during his lifetime, and made divine in the mausoleum after his death.

The monument, situated at the II milestone of the Appian Way (the Via Appia), stood in the center of a large quadriporticus of brick arcading. Impressive in its massive solemnity, it was a round construction, similar in many aspects to the

Pantheon, and stood as an eternal celebration of Romulus, the son of Maxentius, who died in 309 AD, aged only nine.

"This building, which stood outside Rome, near S. Sebastiano, is now a ruin, particularly the internal loggias; but the central section, being very soundly constructed, has survived intact. It is made of brick, without any ornamentation, and it is dark because there are no sources of light other than the door and a few small openings in the four niches […]; the part indicated has a barrel vault, and the central part is a solid pier supporting this barrel vault, in the middle of which is an opening. The central pier is decorated with niches similar to those in the walls." Sebastiano Serlio (1475–1554) was the first to describe it but many other studies and reconstructions were to follow by important architects such as Sangallo, Palladio and Canina, who recorded the ruins with great accuracy and skill in an attempt to understand the sophisticated construction of the buildings.

Today almost nothing remains to be seen above ground, and we can only imagine its original vastness. Only the constructions below ground remain, where a cylindrical drum extends up to the level of the pavement of the cella above. The farmhouse has made use of this as a large terrace, or sort of hanging garden. "As far as one can ascertain, it was made entirely of brick. Of the loggias surrounding the courtyard, only one part is standing. The entrance into the courtyard had a double arcade, and on either side of the entrance were rooms that must have been used by the Priests […]. In the area in front of this temple, up against the entrance to the courtyard, are the foundations of the portico, but the columns have been removed"[2].

From the remains of the old stairs leading up to the entrance one moves into

Facing: small shafts emit rays of daylight into the circular gallery, adding to the evocative atmosphere.

Below: plan and elevation of the mausoleum of Romulus in a drawing by Andrea Palladio.

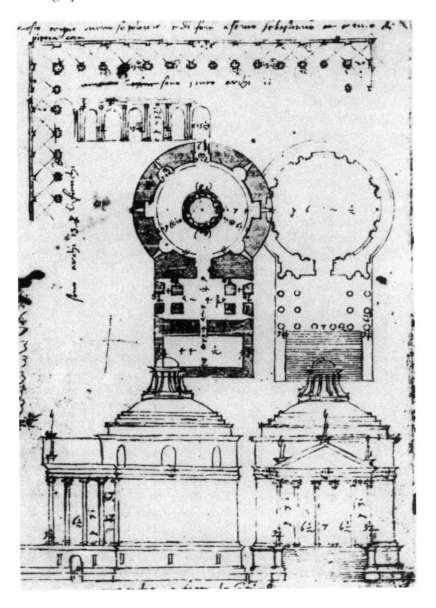

the farmhouse – a rather undignified substitute for the original six-columned pronaos that gave the front elevation of the monument a temple-like appearance. From here it was once possible to reach the cella proper, a circular space surrounded by niches and columns and with a large vault opening to the sky through a large central *oculus*, not unlike that of the Pantheon. There is no trace of this today, and only the hanging garden above gives a hint of its original extent.

A stairway leads inside to a kind of bare vestibule, its rough walls only enlivened by the addition of graffiti and a few later frescoes. A dark and oppressive atmosphere gives us a foretaste of the next room, at the very heart of the tomb. A wide and curving circular passageway draws us along a funerary sacrarium, created as a lasting memorial to the prince who, according to legend, died young by drowning in the waters of the Tiber. An enormous central pier holds up the vault of the ambulatory as if suspended; it is articulated by a series of niches, alternately semicircular and rectangular, which are aligned with similarly alternating niches opposite. Small openings allow light to penetrate, scarcely relieving the austerity and subterranean gloom of the whole. The whole structure evokes a cave, and not even the smoothly plastered walls allow us to forget the mystery of the *spelunca*. Although the vaulted roof and the carved niches – where the arrangement in a seven-fold series may have a sacred significance, a sort of divine numerology – give this underground

cavern an air of having been domesticated, we glimpse in the construction of these passageways a shadowy dimension that is both natural and artificial. It seems as if the artificial has, over the centuries, made way for the natural, leaving it to the latter to gradually reappropriate the work of skilled human hands.

Above: the large central pier, articulated by a series of alternately semicircular and rectangular niches.

Left: fragment of the marble decoration of the complex, today mostly disappeared.

The Mausoleum of Lucilius Peto

Of the original round mound of the mausoleum of Lucilius Peto, only the great marble base with its elegant rusticated blocks of travertine, alternately inverted and the right way up, remains today, situated in a dip in the ground in the ancient "salt street," the Via Salaria.

Emerging from a dip in the land along the ancient Via Salaria, the rounded form of the mausoleum of Lucilius Peto stands as witness to a pride in construction that its present position, low down in the dip, seems to contradict. Proud and majestic, like many Etruscan burial mounds, it stands as testimonoy to the man who found his last resting place here. Its sober dignity is still apparent despite the accumulated earth of centuries[1], and the inscription proclaims its ownership by two wealthy members of the *gens Lucilia*: Lucilius Peto, military tribune and prefect of the smiths and the cavalry, and his sister Lucilia Polla, who had predeceased him.

The elegant inscription[2] on a large marble tablet is placed at the center of the circular drum, surrounded by an ashlar cladding of travertine and forming a compact and geometric section[3] above an elegant cornice. Over the top of this simple and sober design is the conical green mound of earth which gives this

tomb its characteristic structure[4]. It is clearly one of a category of *tomba rotunda* popular in the time of Augustus, and its sober lines and surfaces suggest that it can be dated with confidence to the end of the first century BC.

The imposing appearance of these ancient tombs can best be appreciated by walking around the perimeter. Here we find, concealed within the marble facing of the drum, the original entrance. The small and low arched door leads down a long corridor into the cella, a narrow *dromos* with a plastered roof. The walls show that the space was used at a later date as a catacomb; there are double rows of *loculi* where the original tiles or marble fragments that sealed them are still preserved in some cases. The cavities are, for the most part, small, making it likely that these were mostly the graves of children.

The intense darkness of the corridor leads to the cella, a cruciform structure with three niches. The air is heavy and oppressive. A rapid glance reveals its simple structure, with four protruberances in the corners serving as pillars that support the weight of the drystone vault, and rows of alcoves that clearly reveal their one-time function as receptacles for a *kline*, or funerary bed[5]. We can imagine the recumbent forms, still wrapped in their perfumed white shrouds, and wonder who, besides Lucilius Peto and his sister, found their last resting place here. Taking the rudimentary stairway leading up to the entrance, it is clear from the walls

pierced with a myriad of *loculi*[6] that here was a proper ambulatory of a catacomb, carved out of the tufa, most probably in the first centuries of the Christian era. It is possible that it was done by the descendants of the original patrons of the tomb

who may have embraced the new Christian religion. Thus the monument had a double life, part pagan and part Christian, indicating a continuity of use and survival that is an eloquent expression of its triumph over death.

The Mausoleums of S. Sebastiano

In the labyrinth of subterranean passageways between the III and II milestones on the Appian Way, a kind of palimpsest of memory allows us to trace the many layers of history and the radical changes in ideas about death and the afterlife which occurred.

The consolidated tradition of the *memoria apostolorum*, tied to the cult of Ss. Peter and Paul with its later associations to St. Sebastian, can be misleading, leading us to suppose that this block of sandstone carved out into *loculi* was first and foremost the haunt of catechumens and *fossores*; it might be apparent that here we are looking at the "catacomb" par excellence, an area that, from its proximity to caves, had acquired this name, from the Greek *katà kymbas* meaning "near the cavities." But this earthy mound does not only evoke the Christian martyrs: its complex and many-layered history is witness to the everyday lives of an ancient race. As we plunge below ground, we find a legacy of

elegance very different from the dark succession of catacombs described by Goethe: "The visit to the catacombs, on the other hand, disappointed my expectations: from the first step into these depressing subterranean passages, there awoke in me such an intolerable feeling that I immediately climbed back into the daylight and waited, in that otherwise remote and neglected district, for my companions on the excursion who, being less sensitive than I, had been able to visit even these sites with equanimity"[1]. The oldest indication of constructions on this site dates from the time of the Republic, and consisted of a suburban villa[2] that originally faced onto a lane parallel to the Appian Way. Another smaller villa[3], together with some columbaria, provided evidence of a later building campaign.

But these are not the only remains from pagan times. As one century succeeded another a little cemetery developed, that resulted, after radical alterations sometime in the second

century, from an interment that raised the original level of the floor (9 m. below the pavement of the church) by more than 3 m.

Here there are three small funerary sarcophagi, their fronts still intact, and a funerary chamber covered in frescoes and stuccoes. From the inscription still *in situ*[4] we know that one of the tombs belonged to M(arcus) Clodius Hermes, one was that of the *Innocentiores*[5] and the other is known as that of the *Ascia*, from the axe carved on the front. These three elegant tombs are certainly pagan and date from the later years of Hadrian's rule.

The first on the right (*M.C. Hermes*) presents a hymn to spring and, paradoxically, to life. The frescoes painted on the plastered walls show baskets overflowing with fruit, flowers and birds[6] dancing through an eternal garden of delights, designed to draw the soul of the dead man into a symbolic *paradisus*.

"I would like fruit of every kind to grow around my ashes, and wine in abundance": so says Trimalchio in a famous passage in Petronius' *Satyricon*, a character who is a firm upholder of *post mortem* redemption, where a state of cathartic freedom from life's troubles is reached, in a tranquil attainment of spiritual pleasure. All around, among the dark red octagonal motifs, the story of the funeral must have unfolded: from the oration in honor of the dead man, to the scenes of leave-taking of his wife, of his friends, and of his relations.

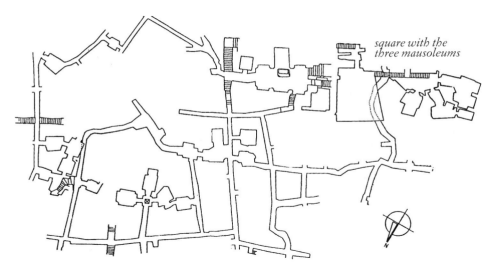

square with the three mausoleums

In the center of the vault, a clumsily painted gorgon's head looks down, and might seem to disturb the delicate, otherworldly dance but for its apotropaic role of providing shelter and protection.

The second mausoleum, known as *Innocentiores*, is faced with white geometric stuccoes culminating in the auspicious embrace of a peacock[7]. The third tomb, built on two storeys like the others, displays an axe, symbolizing the double connotations of a tool and the inviolability of the grave. Like the previous tomb, it is surmounted by an arched vault with a decoration of stuccoed circles and rosettes. The work is executed with great delicacy, reminding us of the importance attached by the living to the preparation of their own funeral tombs. It should be added that in the richness of the grave goods and the decoration, the Romans were seizing a last opportunity to make their mark, to redeem themselves, in this final, and certainly enduring, display of their status.

Above: plan of the subterranean areas of S. Sebastiano showing the little square with the three mausoleums.

Facing: detail of the lunette above the arcosolium. The very fine quality of the work is shown in the skillful painting of the transparent vase, the shadows and the naturalness of the gestures.

The mausoleum of
Marcus Clodius Hermes.

The Pyramid

Right: the Pyramid in an engraving by Piranesi.

Below: the Pyramid of Caius Cestius seen from the non-Catholic cemetery, embedded in the surrounding Aurelian walls. In the background is the Porta Ostiense.

Pyramids, with their steeply tapering sides, have always embodied the idea of an ascent into the heavens, of a staircase leading upwards, taking the soul to its celestial destination. It is for this reason that over time the pyramid has become the funerary monument par excellence. The fascination of its geometrical perfection, of its abstract linearity, has

Above: section of the burial pyramid of Caius Cestius from the western side, in an eighteenth-century engraving.

Facing: view of the pyramid from the same side.

of steps thus merged into the geometrical austerity of the pyramid, conforming to the sense of ritual purity so important to the ancient Egyptians. It is possible that the inspiration for building the pyramid had its origins in the cult of sun worship, in the concept of the monolith, at the tip of which stands the radiant sphere; in the astral worship of the *pietra betilica*, in the belief that this most important sphere was an element of reference both symbolically and for observation, from which the shape of the pyramid developed, with the idea of light flowing from its ray-like form.

In Rome, in the Augustan period, at least four pyramids were erected which were inspired by those in Egypt. Of these, only one survives as representative of the whole category, that of Caius Cestius. There were once twin pyramids in the Campus Martius that stood almost like propylaea at the entrance to the Via Lata, where two churches by Bernini now stand: S. Maria in Montesanto and S. Maria dei Miracoli[1]. In addition, another pyramid stood near St. Peter's, known as the Borgo pyramid, which was destroyed by Alexander VI to make way for his new road through the Borgo. In medieval times, it was identified with ancient legend and associated with the founder of Rome, acquiring the name of *Meta Romuli*, making a pair with the Cestius pyramid believed to be *Meta Remi*. "In the middle of the walls there stands/ a great tomb of huge size/ where Romulus was buried after his death"[2]. This erroneous attribution was not allowed to endure, if Poggio

made it the archetype of man's yearning for the infinite.

The earliest examples are step pyramids (such as that at Saqqarah). Only later did a new style of cladding come to be used, giving the faces of the pyramid a smooth surface, thereby avoiding the unpleasant problems caused by deposits of sand and rubbish carried by the wind, or droppings left by perching birds. The symbolic flight

Bracciolini, with all the passion of a philologist, was correct in his reading and transcription of the name discovered on the inscription on the face of the pyramid: C(AIUS) CESTIUS L(uci) F(ilius) EPULO, POB(lilia tribu), PRAETOR, TRIBUNIS PLEBIS (septem)VIR EPULORUM[3]. Thus, between 18 and 12 BC, Caius Cestius[4], *septemvir* of the *epulones*, which is to say one of the priests of the prestigious college whose duty was to prepare the ritual feasts (*epulae*) for the gods, decided to break with the traditional style of burial monument in favor of a model of clear oriental influence. He built his stairway to the heavens on a vast platform of travertine, facing it with blocks of white luna marble[5].

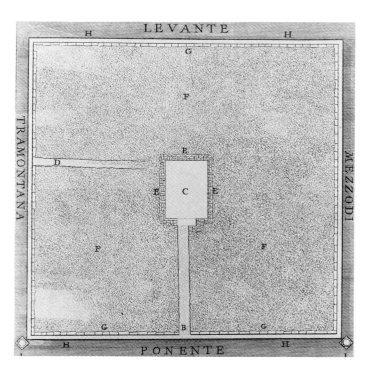

Standing at the crossroads of two important highways of ancient times, the *Ostiense* and the *Vicus Portae Raudusculanae*, the pyramid rises up solemnly near Monte Testaccio, a bulwark of its proud antiquity[6]. Gripped in the embrace of the Aurelian Wall, it recalls, in its verticality, the "Egyptian" fashion of the period; the smooth whiteness of its sides, clad in white marble, invites the viewer to seek a threshold, an entrance. As we step through the small door[7], our eyes find it difficult to adjust to the sudden darkness of the passage after the dazzling whiteness of the exterior. The long narrow corridor seems to be a kind of preparation, almost a cathartic journey towards the final goal: the funerary chamber[8]. Here everything seems very small compared to the massive walls above. Its modest and contained scale, however, emphasises rather than detracts from its fascination.

A sense of unfamiliarity soon fades in front of the reassuring row of graceful female figures painted on the walls. They are reading, carrying sacred vessels or long pipes, emerging from the eroded plaster to keep watch over the deceased with the delicate grace that characterises the art of the "Third Style"[9].

Surrounded by candelabra, vases and grotesques, they seem to shield their eyes from the modern visitor, aloof and rather disdainful in their rich garments. Above, on the vault[10], the figures are lighter and more airy, dressed as Victories and confidently supporting the final apotheosis of

Cestius. Unfortunately, these scenes are only known through old engravings and eighteenth-century drawings, for time and the corrosive effects of the dampness have reduced the elegant composition to a few faint figures, leaving little of this *instauratio funeris*, though enough to indicate its high quality.

Facing: above, plan of the pyramid by Piranesi; below, engraving by the same artist showing the monument as it looked in the eighteenth century.

Below: the travertine cladding of the pyramid makes it clearly visible among the other monuments of Rome.

Columbaria

Here, deep within small cubicles with arched niches, lie the ancient ashes of our past; of hundreds and thousands of men and women who have departed this life. Inscribed over the opening are their names, their ages, what they did, what they loved. Here are painted their faces, the gods they worshipped, their ideas and feelings about the next world, their conception of life and death. The feathery brushstrokes of these painted scenes enliven the network of niches that cover the walls with depictions of the

ancient philosophy of the Romans and, as in a dovecote, abandon the expression of their feelings to that most volatile of elements, the air.

The use of columbaria became widespread in the Augustan period when, as the great mausoleums of the nobility became less frequent, a new type of collective burial, administered by funerary associations, became established, appropriate to the increased population. Its origin is uncertain. The term *columbarium*, coming from the Latin

114 Death

word for dove or pigeon (*colomba*), was coined because of the similarity with a dovecote, with its series of nesting places.

Each niche, or *locule*, could house two or even three funerary vessels containing the ashes of the dead person, making it possible to accommodate many hundreds of burials within the walls of these rooms, thus resolving the pressing matter of overcrowding in the burial places. The system obviously depended upon cremation. The ashes were placed in clay vessels, or, in the case of richer families, in more elaborate urns of alabaster, marble or metal.

On the outer edge of the niche, at the bottom, the name of the deceased was inscribed on a metal strip. The wall around the niche was decorated with delicate ornamental motifs and genre or small mythological scenes which enlivened the space between the niches, bringing a note of light-hearted cheerfulness as an antidote to the sombre subject of death.

These small constructions were mostly well executed, down to the minutest detail, with taste and refinement, resembling a kind of miniature funerary chest in which graceful alcoves with small columns and frontals link the different architectonic parts into a harmonious and varied whole of great decorative effectiveness. The columbaria often belonged to quite modest funeral associations, or to the freed slaves of noble Roman families. Since individual tombs would have been out of their reach, such people would form associations, thus assuring themselves, in exchange for a small annual payment, of a place for their ashes in modest but fitting surroundings.

For the better off, the accommodation was richer and more sumptuous, in columbaria covered with stuccoes and painted walls, the niches dignified and embellished with vigorous little figures painted with delicate brushstrokes conveying metaphorically ideas that were essentially theosophical and transcendental. Characteristic of these paintings is a celebration of nature, overflowing with fruit and flowers inhabited by merry birds and cupids, as evidence of the fertility of paradise; a serene and carefree vision of what awaits the soul in the world to come in the celestial gardens of the Elysian Fields.

With burial, by contrast, the intention was to restore the body to the earth whence it had come. Cremation was linked to ideas derived from neo-Platonism, according to which the soul could free itself through cremation of its "earthly prison" (the body), happy to join once more with the primary matter of its astral constitution.

Facing: niche in the columbarium containing the ashes of Pomponius Hylas and his wife Pomponia Vitalinis. They are depicted in the fresco above, standing on either side of a representation of the mystical cist, as if to declare their belief in the next world.

Below: detail showing Hylas' wife wrapped in a bluish chiton.

The columbaria of Pomponius Hylas

Right: beneath each niche there was always a marble or painted plaque indicating the name, age, and family of the deceased.

Facing: the architectural structure of the columbarium consisted of a dynamic, almost Baroque use of alternating broken pediments and tympana.

Standing apart on its own, in a corner of the Parco degli Scipioni, this minute house passes unnoticed by those visiting the park[1]. And yet a visit to this spot is one that leaves an indelible mark on our memory of the past.

As we step over the threshold and pass down the steep stairway we are drawn in towards the magical oblivion of this tomb. Here, in the delicate beauty of this funerary chamber, we discover another dimension of death, and the journey to the afterlife.

The first thing that strikes us is a warning not to disturb or violate this place. By the stairway, in the facing wall, two griffins before a cithara keep watch over the mosaic inscription indicating that here is the entrance. In fact their presence has an entirely different aim: as apotropaic figures they ward off evil.

Glittering tesserae of glass mosaic spell out the names of those thought to be the owners of the burial place, Pomponius Hylas and his wife Pomponia Vitalinis:

Facing: niche in the left wall of the columbarium. The decoration is enlivened by the bright colors, ranging from blood reds to ultramarine blues and burnt earth.

Left: stucco representation of the centaur Chiron , tamed by Achilles. The cathartic and intellectually improving role of music is symbolized in the depiction of the lyre.

CN(aei). POMPONI HYLAE (et) POMPONIAE. CN(aei). L(ibertae) VITALINIS[2].

When we reach the bottom, there is a surprise. Instead of a dark and gloomy burial place, we find a delicate and exquisite tomb, with a brightly colored background, from which the alternating pattern of the frontals emerges, drawing the eye towards the salient points. Thus, among the dark reds, earth colors and ultramarines, figures and stories emerge, their presence here no chance occurrence, but designed with skill in a hymn to eternity.

Alcoves resembling little temples divide up the walls of a chamber so ornamented that to call it a columbarium would be to diminish it, if not almost to insult it. A better designation would be that of "theater"[3]. Not a theater for tragedy, and even less for comedy, but rather a theater showing the gentle and delicate music of the next world.

In the narrow triangular space of the pediment by the stairway, a stucco Chiron soothes Achilles with the sound of the lyre, extolling the cathartic role of music in a serene representation of the Elysian Fields. Below, in the frieze on the architrave, Ocnus twists his rope as he suffers endless punishment, accompanied by the three-headed Cerberus and a fleeing Danaid, the group apparently referring to the tribulations of Tartarus.

Redemption is celebrated on the vault, in the brightness of the depictions, in the dances of the cupids who clamber among the twining tendrils of the vine. It is almost impossible to unravel the images which, happily occupied amongst the foliage, suggest, in a Dionysiac *humus*,

the delights of eternal bliss. But bit by bit we begin to perceive details, discovering that one cupid is struggling to unroll a scroll, another to walk along a branch, while another, busy reading, seems indifferent to his companion who is swinging on a vine tendril.

In this frescoed minuet of cupids and little birds, the oppressive weight of earth above our heads is lifted up and broken open, in a new and limitless dimension.

Orpheus, with his mysteries, dominates the composition, drawing together the main features of the architecture. On

the central pediment, against a pale blue background, he can be seen in the guise of *Iacchos*[4], leaving his more usual attribution to the frieze below where he seems to be shown near death in the Dionysiac *furor* of the bacchantes. The story, related in a number of episodes, seems to be telling us not to unveil the mysteries, not to try to unravel the tangled enigma of the myth contained within his mystic cist. The figures of the two patrons, the two deceased celebrated in the center of the niche, seem to be indicating the path to take, inviting us to follow. Whether they are Pomponius Hylas with his wife, or Granius Nestor with his wife Vinileia Hedone[5], their expression of farewell and, particularly, their profession of orphic faith seem to make the attribution irrelevant.

As if miraculously, everything seems to be revealed allegorically, conveying its message of participation in the mysteries with clarity and simplicity. The soaring *Nikai* too, suspended from the highest point of the vault, announce their message of triumph over death and, in orphic terms, eternal salvation[6].

Detail of the mosaic on the wall opposite the entrance stairway. The inscription mentions the names of the couple who commissioned the burial place and indicates, with the "v" (standing for vivit*) above the name of Pomponia Vitalinis, that she was still living at the time when the columbarium was built. The two griffins facing one another on either side of the lyre have an apotropaic function, being there to ward off the evil eye.*

The columbaria of Vigna Codini

Three important columbaria, their roofs visible above ground, can be found behind the Porta Latina, far from the din of the busy streets, among the well-guarded villas of the wealthy. Unexpected episodes in this somewhat unusual panorama of swimming pools and sunbeds, they document the history of burials in this area halfway between Porta Latina and Porta San Sebastiano.

Nothing is left of this legacy from the past apart from the columbaria of Vigna Codini, discovered in the first half of the nineteenth century by Marchese Campana and Pietro Codini, who was the owner of the land[1]. Here, three subterranean burial complexes are still to be seen, dating from the Tiberian or Neronian period, in a reasonable state of preservation.

The first columbarium[2], consisting of a large square room below ground level, arouses uneasy feelings. An enormous central pier, pierced with niches, supports the entire massive weight of the vault[3].

Previous pages and facing:
the columbaria of Vigna
Codini. The first
columbarium we reach is
a large underground
quadrangular chamber
supported in the center by
a large pier pierced with
many niches. Another two
rows of jars are sunk into
the bench extending
round all sides of the
chamber.

Left: a light-colored
plaster covers the walls of
the hall. Delicate
decorative motifs with
foliage and birds have
been added, together with
the usual painted
inscriptions giving the
names of the deceased.

Access to the interior is by a steep stairway. Here, there are nine rows of superimposed arched funerary *loculi*. Another two rows of vessels are sunk into the bench that extends around the bottom of the chamber wall[4].

We feel oppressed by the rows of empty niches in this crowded funerary passage, once the last home for a married couple's ashes. This simple place was decorated with lively figures, multicolored birds and flowers, painted with light touches of the brush. It was not just a desire for ornamentation, but rather an attempt to accompany the deceased on their way with this depiction of the celestial garden, to cheer them with the promise of serene and playful joy. The need for spiritual elevation, for catharsis, also lies behind the images. The choice of Dionysiac themes answered this need to believe in a life after death, providing a reassuring response on the matter of our final destiny.

The second columbarium[5] is a large cube, pierced with niches and with a floor of *opus signinum*. Here too the lower part of the wall with the niches was taken up with painted or marble plaques giving the names of the deceased. They were, for the most part, freed slaves of the imperial court who, at their own expense, had this collective tomb built[6] and designed its decoration, creating around the alcoves a series of miniature monuments with architectural niches supported by columns or pilasters in colored marble or stucco. Around them, they commissioned frescoes[7] with lively and joyful motifs twined

around with vegetation, to the sound of Dionysiac cymbals, with baskets of fruit and drinking horns; attempting with these bright depictions to escape from the dismal and gloomy aura of death.

The third columbarium[8], larger and more imposing, is distinguished by its U-shaped plan, with three communicating arms. A double stairway leads to the interior, made oppressive by the weight and dizzy height of the walls[9]. It must once have been elegantly ornamented throughout, the frescoed vaults and walls divided by pilasters with colored marble capitals.

Today it is difficult to imagine this wealth of decoration, for the plaster is very eroded and damp. We can gain some idea of its original appearance, however, from the small fragments still visible on the vault and between the niches. The spaces between the *loculi*, mainly faced in marble, are square in form, allowing space for the urns that we know from the inscriptions belonged to slaves and freemen from the imperial house. These figures from ancient times seem to whisper, invoking the Manes and murmuring their names, ages and station in life. One warning reminds those inclined to linger: "*Ne tangito, o mortalis, revere Mane deos!*" (Do not touch, o mortal, respect the Manes!). It is like an alarm bell that breaks the intimacy of our conversation

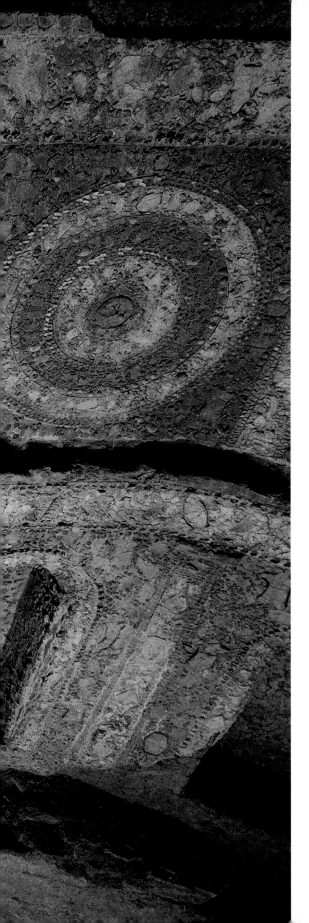

A nympheum is a place dedicated to the cult and veneration of nymphs. Whether Nereids, Naiads or Oceanids, they preside over the clear waters of springs and fountains, ensuring their life-giving and procreative flow: "Fountains and streams belong to the water nymphs"[1]. Homer describes these daughters of Zeus as beautiful maidens, found in glades and clearings where they indulge in their favorite activities of hunting and dancing. They produce and raise heroes, and live in caves where water trickles constantly; interpreting the magic, the message and the force that emanates from that element.

As personifications of the sentiments generated in the contemplation of Nature, they embrace all its manifestations. Young and graceful, they embody the spontaneous feelings of the mind when confronted with the sights and delights of

WATER

Nature. They animate the emotions on seeing intimate natural scenes and are to be found in the peacefulness of hidden valleys, the mysterious recesses of cool woods, the magical solitude of a verdant riverbank or by a babbling brook. Alluring and bewitching, they can be dangerous to those captured by them and seduced by feelings they excite. It was said that anyone seeing a nymph would be rendered insane. Those with mental disturbances were therefore thought to be possessed by nymphs. Anyone carried off by the nymphs would suffer from a fit of madness, or "exalted enthusiasm." One superstition speaks of the madness that infects someone who, part fearful and part fascinated, glimpses a figure coming out of the water. If the nymphs represent Nature in its multiple forms, it is with water and its complex dual symbolism that the Greeks particularly identified them. From water comes the idea of generation and regeneration, for it is the purifying fountain of life, containing within itself the germ of all living things. For this reason, the nymphs were associated with marriage, and particularly with the bridal bath. The custom whereby brides would go to the local river to sprinkle themselves with the water and pray for children was based on a belief in the generative and life-giving powers of water. Girls about to be married were known as nymphs, a word that means "veiled" (with the marriage veil). As lesser gods or semi-gods, nymphs did not at first have temples, but instead sacred places and altars. They were venerated in woods, caves, near springs and fountains, or in other places where their presence was felt. Later, small temples or *nymphaea* were dedicated to them, and these were erected in towns as well as outside; they were used to celebrate marriage ceremonies. For the Romans, the concept of a nymph was rather different. Less accustomed to interpreting the spirit of the cult, they imported it without any real belief, so that gradually the nympheum as temple became the nympheum as pleasure pavilion, a place of physical and spiritual refreshment within the grounds of complexes formed by villas and *domus*. Freed of any sentimental or symbolic connotations, nymphaea became popular in Rome as purely ornamental features, embellished with fountains and decorations that suggested the idea of a grotto, a cave, an immersion in Nature. This was Nature artificially created, and for all the skill and care that went into the execution, it had lost something of its original emotional and intimate vitality.

The Roman nympheum, cool and well-organized, had little to do with the enchantments of the nymphs. Nevertheless, there were times, near fountains and springs, where the ancient magic was still felt, and the original spirit, the *locus nymphae* with its prophetic and exalted properties, could be recaptured.

So we should approach a nympheum with these thoughts – to capture, beneath the fascination of the architecture and ornament, the deep and internal genesis of the place: to find, as it were, the nymph.

The nympheum of Egeria

There could be no better setting for visualizing the lovers' meetings between the beautiful nymph Egeria and Numa Pompilius than in this grotto which bears her name; amid the murmuring waters, in the shade of wisteria and climbing plants, and with the echoes of prophetic whisperings. It must be said that here, more than anywhere else, the myth brings the place to life, while the place gives

substance to the myth. Reached only with difficulty through the huge Caffarella park, and seemingly hidden away so that it will be appreciated only by the more discriminating, the grotto of Egeria embodies the prophetic secrets of the nymph, leaving an indelible impression on anyone who manages to discover it after a long walk through lanes, paths and woods. "There was a wood, supplied with water in the middle by a perennial spring that rose out of a shady grotto. And since Numa came there often alone, as if to meet with the goddess, he dedicated this wood to the Camenae, for they met together here with his bride Egeria"[1].

Visited by foreign travelers like Stendhal and Goethe, the nympheum still casts its Arcadian spell, hidden as it is from the surrounding landscape. It is only with difficulty that the entrance is discovered through the thick undergrowth of the Caffarella that seems to shield it, as if to keep its existence a secret, to preserve a remnant of its mythical integrity.

Inevitably, the past beckons; a time when the followers of Cybele rushed frenziedly, with wild cries, through these cool glades to the throbbing sound of drums. With the arrival of spring, these followers went from the sacrarium on the top of the Palatine hill to the point where the river Almo meets the Tiber, to perform the sacred ritual of *lavatio Matris Deum*: "There is a place where the river

Sculptural detail from the nympheum of Egeria.

Almo flows into the Tiber / and loses its name in that greater River. / The white-headed priest dressed in scarlet robes / there with that water washes the goddess and the sacred objects. / The worshippers cry out: the flutes sound frenetically / the hands of the eunuchs beat the drums"[2]. We can imagine these castrated priests of the goddess – the Great Mother of the Gods – carefully washing the sacred instruments and the black stone, a meteorite from Pessinus that in ancient times represented her effigy and non-figurative simulacrum.

The spell is broken, and the valley returns to its present deserted state. The waters of the Almo, once clear and sparkling, are now reduced to an enclosed ditch, a haunt of rats, with the undignified role of a drain. And yet the valley with its glades, clearings and pools, must once have been a magical place with an idyllic and sacred atmosphere: a *locus amoeni*, the perfect spot in which to build one's out-of-town house. This is what Herodes Atticus (101–179 AD)[3] decided when, coming into possession of his wife's vast dowry, he built between the II and III milestones of the Via Appia and the Asinaria.

A politican of great intelligence, a philosopher, rhetorician and patron, he desired to build this luxurious residence in honor of his young wife, Annia Regilla[4], using the extensive lands that she brought as her dowry.

It was an enormous villa, decorated with porticoes, temples, and sacred enclo-sures. Its unusual name of "Triopion" ("Three-eye") derives apparently from the Thessalian hero Triopas, the violator of the temple of Demeter[5]. The complex, a rural paradise, was sacred to the Manes and to Annia Regilla's tutelary gods of the underworld. Today very little remains of this rich and sumptuous country residence[6]. Among the surviving remains, however, can be included the so-called nympheum of Egeria, built in the second century AD as one of the amenities of the villa.

Once inside the damp grotto, where water oozes from the walls, it is hard to visualize its original appearance, or to remember that this is a man-made cave, so convincingly has it returned to nature. The walls with niches, once clad in *verde antico*, are now covered in mould, the water that drips down running off into channels below.

Nothing remains of the rich marble facing of the walls, or the serpentine pavements, the niches decorated with shells and colored mosaics, statues and porticoes. Nature has reclaimed this place and made it her own, covering it with moss and lichens, canceling out all traces of man's hand and leaving only the soft spirit of the "nymph dear to the gods, who was wife to Numa and his councilor"[7].

The nympheum of the Annibaldi

Lost in the marble whiteness of the walls of the Via degli Annibaldi, a little iron gate deceives with its modest air, concealing from view a delightful remnant from the past made up of torrents and little waterfalls. Once part of a sumptuous villa[1], it reveals a world of delicate stuccoes, smooth colored plaster, glass mosaics, ornamental fountains, murmuring watercourses, and many other things designed to delight the *otium* of its refined owners, who lived here on the threshold of the Empire.

A spiral staircase leads down into the *interior terrae*, into the depths of the hillside, and takes us on a journey that is difficult both physically and spriritually. The visitor must penetrate this rocky gorge and pass beyond the *interior terrae*, relying on rational good sense to overcome nameless fears along the way, until he finds a small nympheum[2]. Here, the vision fuses like an arabesque into alternating shields and pilasters. A carpet encrusted with stuccoes and shells arranged in lozenges, shields and cuirasses marks the passage to the niches, until the picture shifts focus to reveal an apse, cut through at right angles in a modern alteration.

The four niches must have originally been nine, giving onto a much bigger hall, culminating in a beautiful basin, or sacred pool. Sculptures and statues[3] provided, with their flashes of light, a visual contrast to the browns and earth colors of pumice and stucco, in an elegant and harmonious effect, enlivened by the

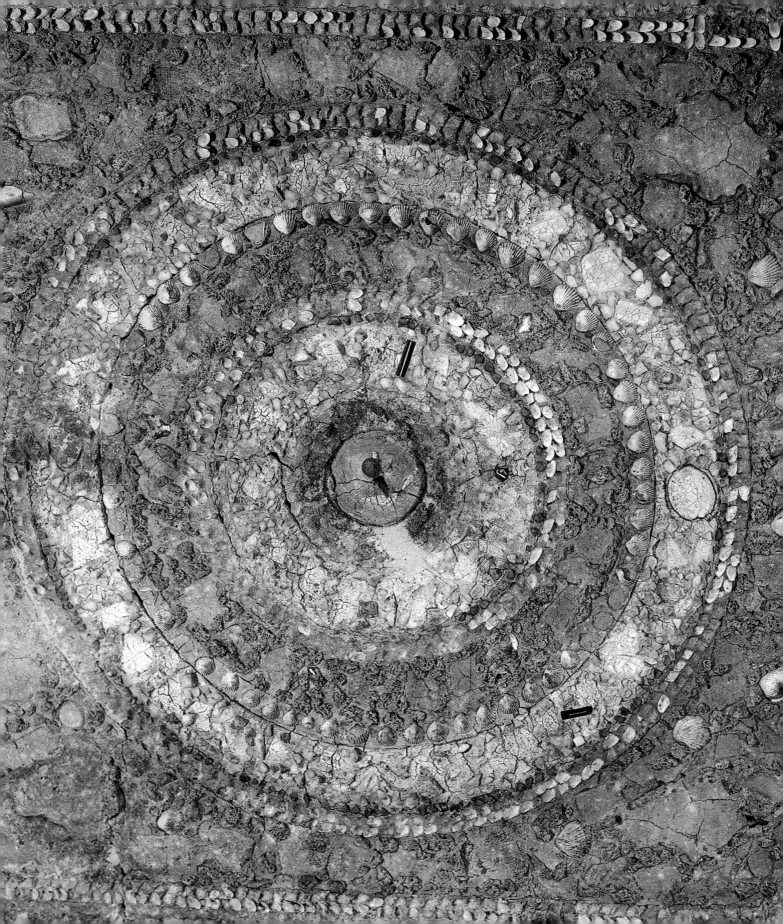

reflections of the water. The cladding of the walls, of *tufa reticulate* made of very small stones, and the exquisite relief work, are typical of the style of decoration of the late Republic. Once inside, however, one forgets the erudition of dating, historical details, their phases and interpolations; as we are transported back to the origins of the myth we discover in the nympheum – the home of the nymphs – their way of interpreting the intimate essence of running water. The *spiritus loci* brings this place alive. Woe betide anyone who allows themselves to be beguiled by the spell of the nymph which pervades it – the enchanting nymph may conceal a witch.

Facing and above: details of the apse of the main hall of the nympheum. The hall must originally have been much larger, but has been reduced by intervening modern building. Of the original nine niches, only four can be seen today, while there is no trace of what was once a beautiful basin.

The *auditorium* of Maecenas

Right: plan of the nympheum, with the entrance (A), the summer triclinium (C), the apse (D), and the vestibule (B).

Far right: detail of a fragment of sculpture exhibited in the small antiquarium laid out inside.

Under a sloping roof, behind the rough surface of its outer face, the *auditorium* of Maecenas[1] hides, almost sulkily, the nobility of its past from the rows of sordid buildings around it.

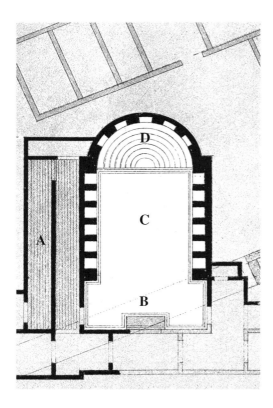

Unaffected, it would seem, by the local traffic and the deafening din all around, it offers a refuge to anyone fleeing the chaos of modern life who might chance upon this peaceful Arcadia, its *horti* and pleasure gardens, made for literary and erudite conversation.

Before Caius Maecenas transformed this area with his *Horti Mecenatiani*, it must have been very different. The hill, once the haunt of thieves and sorcerers, prostitutes and tramps, seemed an unlikely choice for his gardens. But by the time he had finished, Maecenas had restored pride and dignity to the hill. Horace writes: "Now on the restored

Interior view of the hall.

Esquiline one can live and walk in the sun on the bastions, where formerly, with regret, one saw only bleached bones lying on the abandoned ground; and now the thieves and animals that once infested this area no longer disturb or annoy me, any more than do the witches who with philters and spells sought to confuse the human mind"[2].

The villa was surrounded by gardens containing an infinite number of different plants, with statues and buildings, of which, unfortunately, none but the *auditorium* survives. The somber exterior of this last remaining building is the key to the villa's original splendor. A sloping ramp leads down into a long straight-sided hall with an apsidal ending. It is easy to visualize how it must have looked, with the guests reclining on couches and admiring the spectacle of the tumbling waters[3]. The magical notes of the cithara and the flute mingled with the sound of the water; the curtain of water from a waterfall fell in rhythmical sequence onto the variegated green of the Carystian marble steps, draining away in the long channel in the center of the hall.

AN 39

Sheltered from the heat of the summer sun, Maecenas' illustrious dinner guests could refresh both their minds and bodies with odes and songs, while at the same time imbibing the intoxicating Bacchus' nectar. As the symposium became noisier and less formal, we can almost imagine the merry band, who were described by Horace, who "did not deny themselves a glass of old Massico wine, and passed a good part of their day reclining in the shade of an arbutus tree or by the spring where the water of a nymph murmurs sweetly"[4].

Above: one of the surviving sculptural fragments. The very fine execution is evidence of the high quality of the furnishings and decoration of the villa and the Gardens (Horti) of Maecenus.

Left: the painted section of the apsidal wall concentrates on motifs drawn from an idealized nature, with a succession of delicate little gardens enclosed by marble screens and adorned with fountains.

The hall is decorated with trompe l'oeil gardens, a stepped *cavea*, ornamented with plants and flowers, where artifice achieves a sweet naturalism. Plants, birds and fruit painted with light brushstrokes stand out against backgrounds of blues and Pompeian reds. An extensive covering of frescoed decoration[5] clothes the walls with scenes of the natural world, in a celebration – now much muted – of colors and vitality. No matter that the chirruping birds are painted, that the shrubs peeping in at the windows are the product of art not nature: art is the queen of deception.

Looking up from the gentle enchantment of the painted gardens to the dark-colored frieze above, a series of delicate and energetic little figures moving about against a black background can be seen. Light brushstrokes depict satyrs and maenads that emerge as solid shapes from the eroded plaster, allowing us to discover piece by piece faces, features, clothes, and gestures. A goat, stubbornly rejecting Pan's invitation to be sacrificed, makes way for Silenus on a donkey, while further on we see the frenetic dance of the Bacchantae. The scene is a Bacchic procession[6], advancing to the sound of a double flute – the music of Pan. Perhaps some form of initiation was needed, some participation in the Dionysian Mysteries, to make these icons into "signifiers"?

Only after penetrating like this into this secret world, to rediscover its role and the generative force of nature – its birth and

rebirth, its inner mystery – could the supreme values and inspired character be revealed through participation in such a symposium. On entering the hall all would then have become clearer, even the epigram by Callimachus on the outer wall of the apsidal end: "If I approached you while drunk on purpose, O Archinus, rebuke me, but if it was without meaning to, excuse my audacity. Wine and Love had me in their grasp; the one impelled me, the other did not allow me to relinquish that audacity. And when I came I did not understand, who he is and whose son, but I kissed the ground, if this is a fault then I am guilty."

SACRED PLACES

By using the word "sacred," our intention is to approach both pagan and Christian buildings from a common cultural viewpoint. Such a categorization is certainly controversial but, nevertheless, it has the advantage of allowing us to look specifically at temples, shrines and sanctuaries from the point of view of the religious element in Roman culture.

From the conventional pagan sacred areas, and the temples associated with them, to the establishment of oriental sanctuaries, right down to the *titoli* of the Christian era, it is possible to trace a path that leads from the more traditional forms of worship of the pagan *Pantheon*, to the more complex situation with the "crisis" of oriental religiosity, and eventually to Christianity. Although the examples looked at here are few, they exemplify the stages of an evolving journey and an historical continuity towards monotheism, with all its architectural and formal implications.

Previous pages: detail of the mosaic over the painted frieze on the left-hand wall of the hypogeum in the Via Livenza, and a decorative detail from the subterranean complex of S. Martino ai Monti.

Facing: the entrance stairway to the complex of S. Martino ai Monti.

Left: holy water stoup in one of the underground rooms beneath S. Cecilia in Trastevere.

The *area sacra* of the Largo Argentina

Plan of the area sacra *of the Largo Argentina showing the sequence of aligned temples that, in view of the difficulty in identifying them definitively, are indicated by the letters A, B, C, and D.*

At the far end of the Pigna district, a group of old medieval cottages, noblemen's houses and churches once concealed a much older center. It was discovered by chance during the construction of a large modern building in 1918, fortunately never completed.

Excavations revealed a sunken square with a forest of columns, surrounded by trees. Because of its position below the Piazza Argentina this *area sacra* is known as the Largo Argentina.

It consists of four temples standing one behind the other, with a number of altars

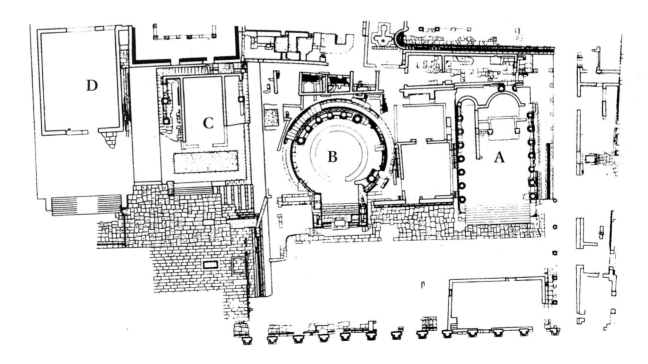

Plan of the area sacra *of the Largo Argentina showing the sequence of aligned temples that, in view of the difficulty in identifying them definitively, are indicated by the letters A, B, C, and D.*

in front, amid the confusion of chaotic and deafening traffic. It is hard to imagine it in the past, in a less stressful time, when it must have been a peaceful and sacred spot.

The temples are known as A, B, C, and D, since their dedications are not firmly established, although many ingenious theories assign a divinity to each temple. The oldest is C (which dates from the end of the fourth and beginning of the third century BC), the third in line starting from the Largo Argentina. Resting on a podium of tufa, it is of the characteristic and archaic sine postico type (that is, with the back of the cella closed). Some scholars suggest that it was a temple to Feronia, an ancient Italianate divinity

who pronounced her prophecies at the foot of Mount Soracte.

The second, in chronological order, is Temple A (the first from the right), the cella of which supports the apses of the small medieval church of S. Nicola dei Calcarari. A peripteral hexastyle structure, it can very probably be identified as a temple to Juturna, built in 241 BC by Lutatius Catulus after his victory over the Carthaginians.

Last in the row and third in order of antiquity is Temple D, still partly concealed from view by the road, the Via Florida, that passes over it. This temple is built entirely of travertine and is generally thought to be the site of the cult of the *Lares permarini*, protectors of the sea's highways.

Temple B, the last, is the largest and most beautiful of the four, with its circle of columns that relieve the rigid axiality of the others[1]. On this site the remains of a huge acrolith of a female figure were found, which have been identified with the *Fortuna Huiusce Diei* ("Good Fortune on This Day"), founded by Q. Lutatius Catulus (a different one, who was consol in 101), together with Marius, following the victory of Vercellae over the Cimbri.

The whole complex forms a large archaeological park that brings together in one area several important temples of the Republican era, forming a religious site that, during the course of the centuries, has undergone considerable change[2], but which still preserves intact its sacred aura.

All these buildings have been considerably altered over time, and these changes have modified to a considerable degree the original structure, which itself revealed a number of different building phases[3]. Often, in fact, inside the temples, at their very heart, there are hidden altars, pavements, podiums and *favissae*, as if deliberately hidden from prying eyes. Beneath the modest cladding of tufa there is an internal nucleus with a labyrinth of underground passageways that open up onto unexpected rents in the innermost fabric of the temple[4], providing evidence of the changes and the different situations that occured on this site. They also tell a story of fires and of social and religious changes, and remind us that beneath this tangle of ruined buildings lies history.

Three temples in the Forum Holitorium

Vegetables were a fundamental part of the Roman diet, particularly for the less well-off. The use of such produce was so common that Plautus, in one of his comedies, portrays a cook who is complaining to his colleagues that he is having to treat the diners like cows, offering them vegetables served with other vegetables. Martial similarly pokes fun at a Romulus who can survive on turnips even in the afterlife. Ovid seems much ahead of his time when he says in uncompromising tones: "It is a crime to heap one's table with the flesh of animals, when we have gardens that produce all the fruits of the earth"[1].

Almost all Romans had a small vegetable garden, priding themselves on what they grew there and obtaining the greater part of their sustenance from it. When the garden could not provide sufficient vegetables, they would go to the fruit and vegetable market, the *Forum Holitorium*[2]. This lay near the port on the Tiber, in the area where there is now a piazza between the slopes of the Capitoline hill, the Theater of Marcellus, and the Tiber, outside the Servian city walls.

The commercial importance of this area was reinforced by the presence nearby of the public granaries (today the site of the registry offices) and the *Forum Boarium* (cattle market). To mark the activity at the latter, there was apparently a bronze statue of the Aegean bull. The Forum Holitorium had instead a marble elephant, known as the *Elephas herbarius* because of its position.

As early as the end of the Republic, the Forum Holitorium had already changed function, becoming a monumental square. It acquired temples and porticoes and, with the inauguration of the Theater of Marcellus (11 BC), it was beautifully paved with travertine slabs. Three large temples with aligned facades occupied the western side of the forum. The first was of modest proportions, of the Doric order, and encircled with columns (peripteral)[3]. The second, in the center, was also peripteral with six columns at the front, but of

Ionic order[4]. Finally, the third temple, also with a facade of six columns, was of an Italianate type of Ionic order, peripteral but *sine postico* (lacking the colonnade at the back)[5]. It is not easy to assign names to each of the temples, but documentary sources make it seem likely that they were the temples of Spes (Hope), Juno Sospita (the Saviour), and Janus.

These same sources mention another temple, that of Pietas (Piety), built to fulfill a vow made by Manius Acilius Glabrio during the battle of Thermopylae. This temple had a short life (from 191 BC to 181 BC), for it was soon demolished to make way for the Theater of Marcellus. Nevertheless, a legend grew up around it

which contributed to the creation of the placename *in carcere* ("in prison") which was added to the name of the church, S. Nicola. The church has incorporated the lower part of the temple of Juno Sospita beneath its floors. Pliny tells the story: "A girl of the common people, and hence unknown, had a mother who was shut up in prison as a punishment; having asked if she could go in, and having been chased away by the guard lest she brought her mother food, she was surprised one day suckling her mother from her own breast. As a result of this miracle, the mother was released and dedicated to the goddess Pietas, as was the place, and both women were granted

Jean Barbault (1705–1766), Ruins of the Holitorium, *watercolor.*

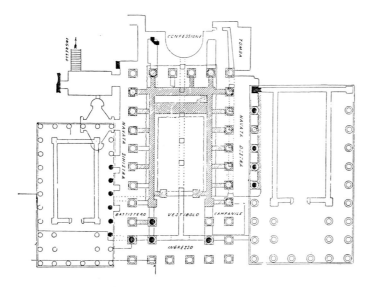

Above: plan of the area sacra showing the alignment of the three temples. It is evident that the church of S. Nicola in Carcere has incorporated the structure of the central temple, extending its aisle walls to swallow up the external columns of the other two temples.

Facing: general view

food for life; this happened during the consulate of C. Quinctius and M. Acilius and therefore the temple of Pietas was built on the site of the prison, where the Theater of Marcellus now stands"[6].

This legend originated in Greece, and was known throughout the Middle Ages, though with the mother substituted by the father. It was so widespread that it provided a source of inspiration for many writers and painters. From Caravaggio to Lord Byron, the story illustrates the theme of charity and mercifulness. The poet Belli, too, was inspired by the story to produce his witty and demythicized version, with a father uncompromisingly depicted as "ugly, old and filthy."

The subterranean areas are reached from the crypt under the high altar of S. Nicola in Carcere. The foundations of the church rest on the central temple of Juno Sospita, while the side aisles extend to left and right into the space between the three temples, its side walls having incorporated the external colonnades of the two on either side[7].

Beneath the left aisle of the church, a long corridor allows us to see on the right the high bases of the six Doric columns of the temple attributed to Spes. To the left can be seen the bases belonging to the middle temple. The passageway is suspended between the two buildings, revealing, at close quarters, all the treasures of temple architecture with its harmonious sequence of spaces and rows of columns, standing on aligned podiums. It is a sight best appreciated by lovers of art and architecture, and especially that scholarly group of Renaissance artists who studied and measured the Antique ruins with such enthusiasm[8].

Halfway along the left-hand wall is a cella consisting of three compartments that has puzzled archaeologists and which appears to have been erected at a later date, possibly in the Byzantine period[9]. Beneath the nave of the church the long hall reveals the bases of the middle temple and in the inner part still preserves the *favissae* (ex-voto offerings). The third corridor reveals the whole of the side of the Italianate Ionic temple, with the bases of the seven columns embedded in the right wall of the church. This does not, however, detract from the genuine evidence of commercial life that once took place around the temples, where small shops sold drinks, sweets or religious souvenirs to the common people.

The Syriac sanctuary on the Janiculum

Not far from a gushing spring, inhabited by the lingering spirit of a nymph associated with the Furies, the remains can be seen of a mysterious and enigmatic sanctuary of Syriac origin[1]. In the nymph's sacred grove, on the slopes of the Janiculum, a cult arose, influenced by eastern beliefs and paying tribute to the evil and vindictive spirit Furrina[2]. It is a sinister place, marked by the dreadful nature of its *genius loci* and by sad and disturbing crimes[3].

It was discovered in 1906, when the excavation campaign uncovered at least three building phases[4], of which only the last is easily interpreted.

On the far side of the Tiber, away from official cults and institutional liturgies, the communities of foreign slaves, freedmen and profiteers introduced their own rites and idols, enriching the traditional pantheon with the complexities of the cults of mystery. In *Regio XIV*, therefore, the transcendental aspirations of the East, with their strongly felt need for redemption and ideas on death and resurrection, found fertile ground. Whether Isis, Dionysus, Mithras or Atargatis, their syncretic mixture was quickly adapted in this area of Rome across the Tiber, far from the constraints of religious tradition.

Axonometric reconstruction of the Syriac sanctuary on the Janiculum. It is formed of three sections, clearly visible on the plan: the main hall, basilical in form, the courtyard, and the octagonal building preceded by a vestibule.

The first emergence of a temple on this spot, in the form of a *tèmenos* with a basin or sacred pool[5], should be understood in this context. The same is true of its subsequent transformation at the hands of one Giaonas[6], a rich and generous Syrian merchant who had brought with him to Rome not only his wares, but also his beliefs and observances. Destruction, or more probably fire, put an end to the first sanctuary. What is visible today is the remains of a remodeled version, with a different orientation, thought to date from the fourth century.

The building must have been a space enclosed within surrounding walls[7] with a courtyard in the center arranged in three distinct sections; a basilica-shaped building to the west, and, to the east, another building of octagonal plan. It has a curious orientation offset by eight steps between the perimeter walls and the inner courtyards, thus correcting the direction of the axis of the temple towards the East, which is to say, towards the rising sun, as sacred tradition requires[8].

The courtyard stood between the two principal areas of the cult: the basilica-shaped building was intended for public ceremonies, while the other hall seems to have been reserved for rituals associated with the mysteries. The basilica-like building has three naves, the middle one wider than those on either side. All three had niches, leading us to presume that three was the number of divinities worshipped here. Since the large headless statue of a seated figure found near the

central apse can, from comparison with similar figures of Syrian origin, be interpreted as Jupiter Heliopolitanus (*Hadad*, or Zeus Sarapis), it is possible that the other two divinities were those that completed the Heliopolis trinity: Atargatis (the Syrian goddess of the Romans) and her son Simios (who became Mercury for the Romans and was in turn associated with Dionysus).

A strange foundation ritual must have been involved in the establishing of this

The wall of the entrance narthex made of opus vittatum *with somewhat irregular reused tufa blocks. Three niches are visible in the back wall.*

*Right: view of the
basilica-shaped hall from
the courtyard. The niches
at the back are clearly
visible, probably intended
to contain statues of the
Heliopolis trinity of
Hadad (Zeus Sarapis),
Atargatis, the Syrian
goddess of the Romans,
and Simios, romanized to
Mercury and associated in
turn with Dionysus.*

*Following pages: general
view*

The bronze idol found inside a triangular altar. It represents a deity with Egypto-Syriac connotations, a syncretic sun god who dies and is reborn.

cult, for a toothless skull, missing the lower jaw, was discovered in a cavity carved out below the niche of Jupiter-Hadad. This object mysteriously disappeared after its excavation. And the mysteries of this sanctuary do not end here. Discovered in the polygonal part of the structure, facing east, were an Egyptian statue in black basalt (from the apse) and another of Dionysus with gilded hands and face. Furthermore, a strange little bronze idol was found, carefully laid out on its back, inside a triangular altar. It represents a youth, embalmed and tightly wrapped, and encircled by the seven coils of a snake that rests its head on that of the figure. When the statue was discovered, seven eggs[9] were found among the snake's coils, arranged in a clearly symbolic way. This extraordinary find created much impassioned research[10] into the idol's identity and role. It is not clear what it represented, although it is certainly a deity with Egypto-Syriac connotations, a sun god who dies and is born again. Simios or Adonis, or perhaps Osiris or Dionysus: the only certainty is that it is a mystery cult associated with the idea of redemption. It is likely that the idol was placed (buried) here in the winter months, and then brought out and exhibited in the spring in a symbolic ritual.

This was the most secret and secluded part of the sanctuary[11], where, in a dark and oppressive atmosphere, the initiation took place of the neophytes[12] of those eastern communties that had introduced into Rome not only their idols but also their belief in salvation.

S. Crisogono

Facing: view of the left side of the apsidal complex of the original titulus, *with the crypt and cella for the holy relics..*

Below: detail of the frescoes found on the northern wall. They showed a cycle with stories of the life of St. Benedict, dating from the tenth century.

The *Regio XIV* – Trastevere – was a vast district on the right bank of the Tiber, inhabited chiefly by Jews and Syrians, but also by a diverse and mainly foreign population of middle to lower classes, employed in the maintenance of the port there, or in associated trading activities. It was a social context that was exceptionally favorable to the development of new forms of Christian ecumenism, concerned above all with liberation and redemption. In this fertile and active social environment, occasions for assemblies and religious reflection were found in the houses of the richer inhabitants. They would offer part of their homes, or sometimes even their entire house, for use by these early communities. The ancient names of the *tutuli*, the ancient basilicas, remaining in Trastevere, are today a reminder of the history of this district, while the wealth of subterranean structures are evidence of the remains of a rich and complex Early Christian period that was to herald an era of active and productive development.

In 1907, when the Trinitarian fathers L. Manfredini and C. Piccolini, investigating the area beneath the sacristy of S. Crisogono, discovered a semicircular wall, they had no idea that they were about to uncover one of the most interesting and unusual Early Christian basilicas.

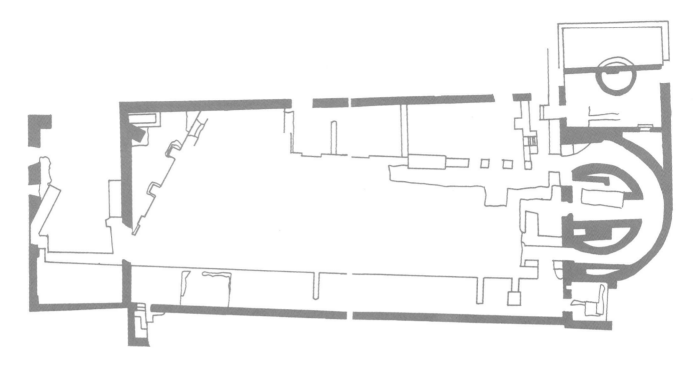

Above: plan of the basilical complex. Clearly visible are the narthex, apse with the crypt and semicircular corridor, the two pastophoria (service rooms used as a sacristy and for the keeping of holy relics).

Right: foreshortened view of the apse wall.

Facing: detail of the frescoes with a cross with diadem, found on the northern wall (c. tenth century).

Fortunately, this first accidental find was followed by other investigations, until the remains of the earliest church and the late Empire structures on which it was built[1], some 6 m. below ground level, were fully revealed.

As the excavation work progressed, the finds included a rich pavement of inlaid colored marbles; and the area of the presbytery with a *schola cantorum* defined the limits of an ecclesiastical building consisting of a single hall[2] (rarely found in Rome) with a portico and apse[3]. It is an unusual building, not only because of its single nave, but also because of two other structures that stand on either side of the apse, an arrangement clearly of eastern inspiration. They were known as *pastophoria*, and used as service rooms. The one to the right is generally thought to have been a *diaconicum*, a kind of sacristy. The other, on the left side, ought therefore to have been the *protesis*, where holy relics were kept[4]. In fact, the discovery in this building of a number of basins seems to indicate that this was not its intended use. In the excavation records there is a note of the presence of a basin "of unusual shape [the one that is still partially visible] cut out of the southern wall of the room, together with other large rectangular basins, forming a system of inter-communicating recipients for water [now disappeared], with channels leading to a broad covered drain"[5]. The existence of these earlier constructions has given rise to the suggestion that there was once

a *fullonica* (laundry and dye-house), quite possible in a commercial and popular district of this kind. Others have maintained that the basin cut into the southern wall of the room[6] was used for baptism by immersion. It is, of course, possible that the basin served both these functions, first one and then the other. Whatever the truth, what is interesting is the continuity of use of these buildings, and their day-to-day functionality.

When the basilica was built, the building on the left-hand side was given a more monumental appearance with the addition of doors and windows. The rectangular basins were filled in, while the central one was embellished with a rich marble cladding, possibly with the intention of using the room for baptisms. Perhaps it was here that the early Christians were immersed, according to an initiation ritual that fitted well within the devotional and cultural context of the time. They would have been strengthened in their faith by the presence, it is thought, of the first of the apostles who, by transferring his dwelling to Trastevere, to the heart of the Jewish quarter, had made a large number of converts.

The *domus* took its name from Chrysogonus, the *conditor tituli* (founder of the original church). He appears to have been neither a martyr nor a saint, but simply one of the many devout patrons who offered their own houses as meeting places for the early communities[7]. Nevertheless, it was not long before the *titulus Chrysogoni*[8] became *titulus Sancti*

Chrysogoni, giving the owner not only a halo but also an aura of sanctity.

The descent into the depths of this ancient *titulus*, where a sense of the dawn of Christianity is still felt, cannot fail to move us. A stair leads down to a horseshoe-shaped passageway that ran below the apse, forming a crypt. The straight section of this *confessio* was entirely covered with paintings, of which all that survives today are three hieratic figures of saints[9]. These date from the restorations

Above: view of the side of one of the sarcophagi preserved in the left part of the hall, with the carved image of a sphinx.

Facing: detail of the frescoes found on the northern wall.

Below, facing and following pages: one of the sarcophagi situated in front of the sacristy, and one of the most beautiful. It is a depiction in high relief of a procession of sea creatures, including tritons, and nereids who are singing and dancing.

carried out under Pope Gregory III (731–741), who made extensive alterations to the basilica, raising the presbytery[10], renewing the roof and having the walls decorated with frescoes. It is still possible to see the beautifully painted paneling of the apse wall, where disks alternate with lozenges and other more unusual geometric shapes. The cella for the holy relics, the true focus of religious devotion, was created in the crypt. From here, through two *fenestellae confessionis*, the worshippers would push their white garments, attached to long sticks, into the room to touch the relics, hoping in this way to acquire something of their sanctity. This was clearly an instance of thaumaturgic contact with the remains of dead saints, a way of capturing their aura of divinity.

Continuing along the passage, a number of interesting sarcophagi provide evidence that some parts of the basilica were used for burials[11]. Moving within the single nave, one has the impression that there are three, since the space is divided up by the foundation walls of the upper church. Here and there the rough walls bear traces of frescoes. On the right-hand wall, not far from the inside of the facade, it is just possible to make out the remains of a cycle of paintings depicting the life of St. Benedict, arranged in two rows, with the usual frieze of draperies below[12]. It can be reasonably assumed that the rest of the basilica was similarly decorated with frescoes, and is an indication of the rich decorative schemes of these Early Christian churches in Rome.

S. Cecilia in Trastevere

*Right: sculptural fragment
in the small antiquarium.*

*Facing: vestibule leading
into the underground
rooms, converted into a
small antiquarium.*

S. Cecilia in Trastevere, showing the strati-
graphic superimposition of the different
periods of Rome's history, is a true
palimpsest of the traces left by time.

The oldest level – first discovered in
1899 when improvements were being
carried out to the crypt – reveals a
dwelling place from Republican times that
was enlarged and altered to incorporate
another house of the same period. These

Underground structure of S. Cecilia in Trastevere. A number of amphorae were found in front of the shrine. The changes in masonry styles provide evidence of the alterations made over the course of time.

changes, which occurred from the time of the Republic up to the fourth century AD, transformed the original nature of the place so that some scholars have suggested – given that none of the elements usually associated with a typical *domus* are present – that the whole complex should be seen within the context of the commercial and artisan area on that side of the Tiber. The presence in one of the buildings of eight brick basins would seem to add weight to this theory. Basing their interpretation on two inventories from the pre-Constantinian period – the *Curiosum* and the *Description of the Regions* – some scholars have presumed that the complex was a *coriaria*, or tannery. It is true that the *XIV Regio*, Trastevere, had developed a commercial character from Republican times.

The proximity of the river and the enlarging of the new port of the *emporium* had led to the development of a settlement made up chiefly of artisans, small traders, millers (there were many mills on the river), workers and immigrants from the east (of which the Jewish community was by far the largest).

The research and investigations that have been carried out to date (even the most recent) do not allow us to identify any of these sites as the house ascribed by tradition as the setting for the martyrdom of S. Cecilia. The presence of a heating system (hypocaust) in the so-called *balneum Caeciliae* is insufficient evidence to support the tradition, particularly since the relevant *passio* (life of the saint) dates from the late fifth century AD and

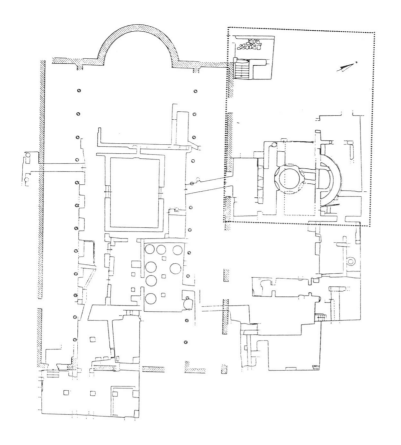

Above: plan of the archaeological area with the basilica.

Below: detail of a mosaic.

Facing: small detail of a decoration

therefore cannot be taken as a reliable historical source. Nevertheless, in these spaces, by the fourth century AD part of a single complex, there is evidence of the presence of a Christian community, or rather of a *titulus* that took its name from that of its founder.

A recent study has shown a continuity in the relationship between the saint and a pagan cult of archaic origin, the *Bona Dea*, active near to the church. The character of this divinity, confusing and mysterious – especially in the rituals – was associated particularly with the charitable healing of the sick. She was usually described as *Oclata, restiturix luminum*. This attribute of "restorer of sight" establishes a link with the name of the saint (Caecilia and *caecitas*, meaning blindness). On the basis of a number of prayers recited in ancient times in the basilica of S. Cecilia in Trastevere (that use terms such as *restitutor*) it has been possible to establish the existence of a sort of appropriation of the qualities of the pagan divinity by the Christian saint[1].

The subterranean areas are reached from the sacristy, and open into a broad space, described as the peristyle of the *domus Caeciliae*. The difference in wall cladding indicates the transformation and alterations carried out in the building as a whole. A gloomy and ancient atmosphere, added to by the inscriptions, sculptures, *plutei* and fragments on the walls all around, gives the area the feeling of a small *antiquarium*, prefacing a journey suspended between paganism and Christianity. A labyrinth of rooms and corridors connected by walls, piers and patched repairs are evidence of the upheavals and complications of its building history. The pavements, too, arranged on several layers and made of a number of different materials and styles,

are indicative of this complicated architectural development. From a rich polychrome geometric pattern we pass to a less remarkable flooring of *opus spicatum*, and then to a refined and elegant tessellated pavement. A sort of corridor then leads, on the right, to one of the most interesting rooms of the complex. It is rectangular, enclosed by a solid brick wall, and has seven circular basins of brick sunk into the floor[2], evidence that this room was used for tanning leather.

Continuing along the passageway, we descend into a large space[3] containing some beautiful fluted sarcophagi and other interesting finds. This room leads into another, one of the oldest of all. At the end of the room, the wall of tufa blocks and the Doric column standing before it give an idea of its antiquity. Lying together on the floor are innumerable amphorae and vases, and tucked into a small niche in the room opposite is a shrine to the Lares. With the discovery of the intimacy of an ancient *domus*, the scene is no longer dark and severe but transformed into one of warmth and welcome. An archaic outline image of Minerva with helmet and scepter accompanied by a maenad and a scene of sacrifice is modeled in simple clay.

At the end of the corridor a narrow passageway to the left contains two tufa columns from the earliest period of the complex, marking the furthest limit of the building in this direction. Continuing along the corridor, the scene changes and opens out into a space of unusual

richness and color. A forest of little columns support *velaria* decorated with stuccoes and studded with mosaics. This neo-Byzantine crypt was created at the beginning of the twentieth century to facilitate the veneration of the martyr's relics[4]. It is a lively and eclectic composition that seems to offset the almost palpable gloom of this subterranean world, but it creates no real emotion. It is no more than an ornamental parenthesis in a place of somber and proud antiquity.

Facing: the niche with the shrine (lararium). *The image of the figure of Minerva with helmet and scepter is cut into the surface of the clay. On either side are a maenad and a scene of sacrifice.*

Below: detail of the hall with the cylindrical basins of brick, probably used in the process of tanning leather.

S. Clemente

The church of S. Clemente, with its many-layered subterranean areas, provides the most important example of the different strata of growth of the city.

The lower areas are reached down a large staircase decorated with a rich array of archaeological finds and lapidary material, leading first to what must have been the narthex of the ancient *titulus Clementis*[1].

St. Clement was the object of great veneration and the subject of many stories collected in the *Letteratura Clementina* and in the *Acta* of the fourth century. From these apocryphal sources we learn that Clement, condemned to exile in the Crimea in the time of Trajan, set in train an intense missionary activity, for which he was punished by the Romans by being tied to an anchor and thrown into the sea. A little later, the seas rolled away to reveal a little island, with the magnificent tomb of Clement, built by angels. Thereafter, the sea rolled away every year to reveal the tomb.

This miraculous event is illustrated in the frescoes on the walls of the narthex, painted by an unknown artist of the late eleventh century. The colorful story

narrated in the *Acta* is conveyed in wonderful detail in two striking panels. From the story of the child who is swept away to sea after visiting the saint's tomb and is then miraculously found again, to the translation of the saint's body, the events of Clement's life follow one another in cinematic sequence, recording the story with great creativity and sensitivity. The dedication is here, and the portrait of the donors, one Benone de Rapiza and his wife, Maria Macellaria, with their children Clemente and Altilia, who are shown commending themselves to God's mercy with their gift[2].

From the narthex beautiful openings lead into the nave and its magnificent remains. The eastern corner of the nave, to the left as we enter from the narthex (the church's apse is to the west), is the most richly frescoed and is evidence of the breadth of the painter's repertoire, moving away from the formalism of Byzantine art towards a more popular and lively style.

On the left, it is possible to make out a number of scenes from the New Testament: an Ascension (or possibly Assumption) with a space for the relic; the Crucifixion; the Holy Women at the Tomb; the Marriage at Cana; and the Descent into Limbo. These ninth-century frescoes fail to arouse our enthusiasm in the way that those nearby, of the eleventh century, showing scenes from the life of St. Alexis, are able to do. As a young man, the Roman Alexis ran away from home on his marriage day. On his return, after years of

wandering and living as a hermit, his father, the senator Euphemianus, does not recognize him but takes him on as a servant, allowing Alexis to live below the stairs in his house for some seventeen years. At the end of his life, the saint writes a letter to the pope telling his story. The pope tells the story to Alexis' father and his wife. This touching story, most vividly

illustrated in the lower church, immediately struck the imagination of the faithful.

Further along the left wall of the nave is the legend of Sisinius, a Roman prefect who tried to arrest St. Clement while he was saying mass, but who was struck with sudden blindness. In the sequence below we see Sisinius's servants, also blinded, attemping to carry off a column,

Above: detail of the bas-relief on the sarcophagus, showing the myth of Hippolytus.

Facing: scene showing the mass of St. Clement, in a fresco on the left wall of the central nave of the lower church.

mistaking it for the pope. The episode owes its notoriety to the colorful comments of the servants: "*Fili de la pute, traite, Gosmari, Albertel, traite. Falite dereto colo palo, Carvoncelle!*" ("Come on you sons of whores, pull! Gosmari, Albertello, pull! You Carvoncello, lever it up with the pole!"). These colloquial remarks are commented on by St. Clement in a laconic judgement in Latin in the upper band of paintings: "*Duritiam cordis vestri. Saxa trahere meruisti*" ("Because of the hardness of your hearts it is right that you have to carry stones"). This repartee between the learned language of Latin and the Italian of the common people echoes the contrast between the illustrated scenes of the saint's life and those showing the more "servile" below, and shows the innovative spirit of the artist and his efforts to give a narrative development to the hagiographic scenes.

The double apse, roman and medieval, that ends the nave is worthy of note. From here it is possible to walk round the intriguing space between the two walls. In the right aisle, an austere enthroned Madonna, surrounded by Byzantine saints wearing diadems, can be found in a niche (eighth or ninth century). Our attention is more immediately captured, however, by a large first-century sarcophagus, with scenes from the story of Phaedra and Hippolytus sculpted in high relief. In the left aisle, apart from a modern altar of Ss. Cyril and Methodius[3], there is also a circular structure that has been interpreted as an ancient baptismal font for full immersion, but which may equally well have been a fountain or even a wine-press.

The level below (the third) is reached from the right aisle by a steep stairway that leads into a maze of rooms of the Roman period (first century AD). They lead from one into the other. In this labyrinth it is not clear where our steps are leading us, but, with the help of a plan, it is possible to find the "palazzo," believed to belong to Flavius Clemens, where the Christian *titulus* was to become established.

Beyond the dividing passage is a large rectangular structure, built of blocks of tufa supporting brick walls built on travertine. On the other side of the passage a less imposing building, possibly an *insula*[4], is subdivided into small rooms arranged around a courtyard, which at one point was to be occupied by the mithraic temple.

S. Clemente, lower church. Fresco in the main nave showing the Mass of St. Clement. *The fresco forms part of an eleventh-century cycle, full of lively narrative detail, illustrating the miracles of St. Clement. Some very interesting inscriptions, written – for the first time – in the vernacular, appear here, and include the names of the donors.*

S. Martino ai Monti

Watched over by the medieval Capocci towers, the church of S. Martino ai Monti with its apse is on the top of the Esquiline Hill, its walls standing on solid and massive blocks of tufa from the Servian Walls. Its arrangement is typical of the historical and architectural *continuum* in Rome from the Imperial age until today.

The stratification of the levels – beginning with the third century AD – is of particular interest for the history of early Christianity, for it was probably here that the original *titulus Equitii*, or meeting house run by a Christian named Equitius[1], was established. It was one of many such pastoral meeting places in Rome created in the early years of Christianity.

From the period of Pope Fabian (236–250 AD), the need to have places of assembly available became such that some seven pastoral districts were organized in the city. As time went by, this subdivision led to the creation of *tituli*, or "titular churches"[2]. When the cult of the saints became established later, the origin of the churches and the names of the families of the founders was forgotten, and gave way to the dedication of the churches to saints, giving them the names by which we know them today. Sometimes the *Domus ecclesiae* was acquired by the community that gathered there to pray, although some traces indicate that they were inhabited by the clergy.

The *titulus Equitii* was situated below the church of S. Martino ai Monti and can be reached from the crypt. It is not known whether it was established on the site of a pre-existing building (some scholars suggest that there was a covered market here), or whether it emerged in the third

century in answer to the needs of the cult. The first references to it appear in the *Liber Pontificalis*, where we read that there was a Constantinian *titulus* on this site linked to the name of the pope, Sylvester, whose well-known deeds are illustrated in the lively narrative scenes of the frescoes in the oratory of the church of the SS. Quattro Coronati. The latest references date from the eighth century, after which the memory of this original *titulus* is lost. It was not until the seventeenth century, during restoration work, that the buried *titulus* was uncovered by the then prior of the monastery of S. Martino. The excitement surrounding this discovery was so great that Cardinal Barberini decided to have copies of all the frescoes made for a volume that is still in the Vatican Library (Cod. Barb. Lat. 4405).

The subterranean area appears today as an irregular rectangular space, oriented almost exactly east-west. Two rows of large piers subdivide the hall into eleven bays in which it is possible to distinguish at least three types of masonry, corresponding to a similar number of building periods. The hall was not originally subdivided as now, but would have been a large rectangle with a beautiful mosaic pavement of black and white tesserae arranged in a check pattern (still visible in places). The whole room was plastered and covered with frescoes, with an adjoining courtyard (partly visible to the north-west). The complex would have had two upper stories (later demolished), one of which would also have been below ground level. It may have been a large block of houses, a rich *insula* with luxurious apartments, or perhaps a covered market. At some point[3], the building underwent a profound transformation towards a Christian function. Small fragments of painted plaster indicate that there were frescoes showing the life of Christ, while the entire inner walls were faced in marble[4].

The devotional and religious function of the building was maintained even after the construction of the upper church and the monastery (ninth century), bearing witness to the vigor of the original legacy.

SS. Giovanni e Paolo

Right: on the lowest level of the underground rooms a small area for bathing has been found. The suspensurae *below the pavement and a basin in the middle of the room still remain.*

Facing: one of the corridors leading to the cella that contained the holy relics.

On the slopes of the Celian Hill, traces emerging from the walls along the roads and streets reveal links with the past.

Beneath the arches of the *clivus Scauri*[1] we are suddenly taken into another time, where warm golden brick is interspersed with the dark brown of peperino, redolent of the Dark Ages. But this extract from the history of the late Middle Ages points to an even earlier time, whose *insulae*, *domus* and workshops were later transformed into Early-Christian and Baroque buildings – witnesses to the footsteps of history.

The medieval buildings merge with those from the Roman period in a happy symbiosis that makes up so many Roman streets, in a harmonious composition of centuries. Thus the brick masonry and relieving arches visible on the outer walls of the church of SS. Giovanni e Paolo open up a vision of the daily life of an earlier time, telling the story of the simple life of ancient communities prepared to accept a new cult from the East with a single god.

The aged wall invites us to enter the church and continue our exploration. The church protects us on our journey, and guards the memory of the history of the original *titulus*[2], associated with a certain Pammachius, *vir eruditis et nobilis*, who died in 410. The church seems to hide any evidence of its ancient past behind its covering of Baroque magnificence. If we persist, we will discover, behind an apparently insignificant door, the past history of this place. Stepping over the threshold, we leave

The nympheum with basins, with a large fresco on the back wall. The theme of the painting, while obviously marine, is not fully identified. Some scholars say that it shows the return of Proserpine from Hades, while others see it as a cycle about Venus. It is one of the best examples of Roman painting between the end of the second century AD and the beginning of the third.

behind the brightly illuminated nave above and, in complete contrast, enter a crowded and dark labyrinth of rooms, arranged on different levels, stretching back through the subterranean body of the church.

This complex of contructions[3] is basically a large *insula* that subsequently, at the beginning of the third century AD, annexed other earlier buildings. After this phase, the complex passed into the hands of a single owner[4], at which time signs of

Christian worship begin to become apparent. The frescoes of pagan subjects were covered over and between the two *domus* a small chamber was created – probably a *confessio* – decorated with frescoes showing scenes of martyrdom.

The intricate complex of rooms succeeding one another can be reduced to three phases of construction: the pagan Roman house[5], the pagan Christian house, and the early medieval oratory. The first room we come to contains basins indicating that this was a nympheum. The large fresco on the back wall, against a colored background, shows an unidentified legendary episode: the return of Proserpina to Hades, or, more likely, a cycle telling the story of Venus, with the goddess accompanied by Peitho and Bacchus[6]. Against a decorative painted background, two female figures are depicted on a rock, one draped in robes and the other naked but arrayed in jewels. The two women appear to be receiving the homage, or greeting, of a male figure shown turning towards them with a cup in one hand and a bunch of grapes in the other. The scene takes place against a background depicting the sea, where cupids in boats are busily occupied with a variety of activities. The meaning of this vivid celebration in blues and ochres, with splashes of vermilion, is far from clear, but it is the largest painting from ancient Rome in existence today, one of the finest products of Roman painting from the turn of the second century AD.

The decoration[7] of the neighboring triclinium is equally interesting. The painted vault is decorated with cupids gathering in the grape harvest, supported by a cortege of *genii* whose shapely limbs are veiled by long cloaks. Peacocks, thrushes and cocks enliven the composition, flying up into the air or dancing in a rhythm echoed by the *genii*.

The next room, thought to be a *tablinum,* has simply decorated walls with a decorative series of trompe l'oeil marble panels, in contrast to the vault whose decorative scheme is clearly inspired by Christianity. Apostles and pairs of animals face one another in a series of curved bands, as if rotating on a catherine-wheel. Figures in togas with scrolls, either prophets or apostles, correspond closely to the iconographic tradition, as does, apparently, the depiction of the *mulctra*, or bucket of milk placed between two sheep, a symbol both of solace and of the life-blood of Christ. If there was any doubt before, the Early Christian origins of these paintings are confirmed by an *orans* (praying) figure who holds his arms out in a gesture emulating Christ's sacrifice (fourth century AD). A step then leads up into the small square *confessio* connected with the tomb of the martyrs and visible to the faithful through the *fenestella confessionis*. The story related by the frescoes here takes us

Below: details of the frescoed decoration of the tablinum that covers the walls within a framework of trompe l'oeil marble panels. The vault, by contrast, has a composition that is of clearly Christian inspiration.

Below: detail of the frescoed decoration of the triclinium.

Facing: detail showing a fantastic animal, half goat, half fish.

back to the very heart of the ancient liturgy, as we follow the progress of the martyred Sts. Crispin, Crispinian, and Benedicta, imprisoned by the soldiers and then decapitated. The drama of martyrdom is followed by that of celestial intervention, while on the fresco on the back wall, showing Sts. John and Paul and the Savior in the *orans* attitude, worshipped by the faithful, the promise of the paradise to come is held out.

Turning back, we discover a stairway leading down to the *thermae* (baths)[8]. Everything seems more oppressive and gloomy, even this place that was intended for physical and mental refreshment. It is hard to recapture a sense of the original pleasures that were once represented by these mosaic pavements, purificatory basins, and hot steam baths.

monument generally known as the "hypogeum of the Via Livenza."

Its discovery in the 1920s caused great excitement. Work was under way on the foundations for some new buildings; as the diggers moved forward, stretches of a wall of brick and tufa blocks began to emerge. At first little attention was paid to this, because of the depth and its poor state of preservation. It was only when a beautiful statue appeared, headless but clothed in rich draperies, that excavations started. Gradually other fragments of statues began to emerge and, most important of all, a unique building, richly decorated with mosaics and frescoes, with an unusual cruciform plan and a hall 21 m. long and 7 m. wide.

The hypogeum is reached down a dark and narrow stairway, with most of its original steps still preserved – thereby confirming the site's original underground construction – which leads to a room[1] containing a large basin, not very wide, but quite deep, separated from the rest of the room by a beautiful marble screen. The air is damp and heavy, but the feeling of unease this arouses is dispelled by the sight of the iridescent colored glass mosaics of the back wall. Whites, reds and blues combine in a chromatic dance heightened by rapid splashes and touches of paint, creating an impressionistic picture of wonderful freshness and vitality. In the center is Artemis with her bow and her deer, delicate in features and form, but determined in her gestures. Mistress of the woods and forests, she is protrayed as a queen, with a diadem and laurel wreath. She is depicted against a wooded background at dusk as she draws an arrow from the quiver, startling a stag and a hind. Inevitably, we are reminded of Homer's lines: "I sing of Artemis with her golden arrows, the sacred virgin, the archer who strikes deer with her darts, sister of Apollo with the golden sword, she who bends her bow of pure gold over the shady mountains and the windswept peaks, carried away with the joy of hunting, and sends the arrows that wound us"[2].

On the opposite side of the room, facing the goddess, is a young nymph of her company – painted with rapid brushstrokes – caught at a moment of repose as she leans on a spear and turns with tenderness to stroke a deer.

Plan of the monumental complex.

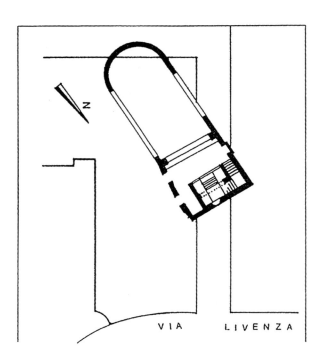

VIA LIVENZA

This Arcadian composition is divided by a painted niche – originally intended to contain a statue – painted with trompe l'oeil Numidian marble (*giallo antico*). This geometric section is interrupted by the magic of a flowering garden where two doves quench their thirst at a fountain (*kantharos*).

The quality of the painting, although lively and impressionistic with its patches of color, is not outstanding, though the rendering of the landscape is effective. The narrative, however, is successfully rendered with freshness and vitality.

The enchantment woven by these colors distracts us temporarily from the other point of interest in the room, the sunken basin. It is rectangular and deep, with steps leading down for immersion. On the first step (1.15 m. down from ground level) we can make out the (reused) tomb inscriptions of soldiers of the Praetorian Guard. Opposite, there is a hole draining away the water and, next to it, a curious opening with a cover to make the water run down. At first sight everything seems to point to a nympheum. But the dampness of this inhospitable site, with its long (21 m.) and narrow hall, suggest that this is unlikely[3].

The supposed nympheum is situated, moreover, in the middle of an area dense with burials, making use of some of the material from the tombs. Then there is the basin that seems rather unwelcoming, both on account of the screen and because of the long reach down to the first step. Further clues may emerge from

some of the little frescoed scenes that appear in the band immediately above, with little putti busily engaged in a variety of different games and fishing activities. One is swimming along, dragging a swan by the neck. The swan is flapping its wings to free itself from this infantile

To the right of the central niche, perhaps intended to contain a statue, is the image of a young nymph, captured in a moment of repose as she turns tenderly to caress a deer.

abductor. Another cupid, sitting comfortably on a rock, is amusing himself by spearing some unfortunate fish or octopus on his trident. Others move across the water with boats and fishing nets, accompanied by aquatic birds. It is a marine scene – of which there are many surviving from antiquity – acting as a frame to the mosaic above it[4].

The mosaic, made of polychrome glass tesserae, is no longer complete. With difficulty we can make out, in the lower part, two figures, one standing and the other kneeling before a rock from which emerges a gush of water.

At first sight it seems as if we are looking at the well-known biblical story of St. Peter who, like Moses, makes water flow from a rock, but this time to baptize the converted centurion. If this is the case, this would be one of the earliest examples of a Christian baptistery for baptism by immersion[5]. But how then can we explain the presence of Diana the Huntress? What role can she have in a temple of initiation to Christianity?

In an attempt to solve this riddle, some scholars have explained the figure of Diana the Huntress as a symbol of paganism who drives the deer (the probable Christians) away from the baptismal font and kills them. The nymph caressing the deer thus symbolizes a figure benevolent towards Christianity, a kind of *nympha sancti Petri*, and is seen as having links with a well-known site on the outskirts of Rome: *ad nymphas Santi Petri ubi baptizavit*[6].

This interpretation is ingenious, but seems to involve twisting the evidence, since comparisons and textual evidence do not seem to support the suggested Christian symbolism attributed, for the first time, to Diana or one of her nymphs.

So what kind of building can this be? What mystery is concealed behind these curious images? More attractive, but equally daring and unsubstantiated, is the theory that this was once a sanctuary for a mystery cult that had as a central feature of its rituals a plunge or immersion into water. The devotees of one such cult, well-known for their dissolute behavior, were known as *Baptai*, from *bapto*, "I immerse"[7]. The plunge into water was a form of liberation, like a change of state of an inspired type. The term *Baptai* means "immersed in water" or practising *baptisma*, and the group, with its clearly orgiastic connotations, had as its principal deity the Thracian *Bendis*, defined by the more forthright as a "coarse demon", and by others as "guide of the shameless."

Supporting the hypothesis that the site was used by such immoral assemblies is the fact that the goddess Bendis (often associated with another Thracian goddess, *Kotys*) was assimilated – and we have the evidence of Heroditus to support this – with the Greek Artemis[8]. Of all the hypotheses, however, the most likely would be that which sees the site as an "ordinary" nympheum, a place that today, squeezed in behind a garage, is still waiting for the recognition that its complete identification would secure.

Facing: frescoed band on the left wall. Against a deep blue background, little putti are busy fishing or playing games.

Hypogeum of the Flavians

One of the most extensive Roman catacombs contains within it a Roman tomb that is traditionally said to be that of the Flavians, a Christian family of the imperial period.

This grandiose tomb is one of the oldest and most interesting elements of the cemetery of Domitilla and was discovered in 1865 by Michele Stefano de Rossi[1]. His account is enthusiastic: "Convinced that there must be a Christian cemetery here, I wanted to descend beneath the ground from the Sacripanti vineyard that occupies this small rise. The reader will imagine my joy when, after telling the workers to dig here in search of an entrance to the subterranean chambers, they found a hole, and, after a short time, an opening appeared down which ran a magnificent stairway, the walls of which were all plastered and painted with frescoes."

In ancient times the cemetery was approached by a public road that led to a facade with an outer wall in fine yellow and red brickwork with projecting cornices, of the kind also found in the so-called "piazzola" of S. Sebastiano and in other tombs in the necropolis of the Isola Sacra[2]. At a later date, this was covered by a long rectangular vestibule, flanked by two low benches.

Today the site is approached from inside the gallery that is linked to the maze of passageways forming the complex. It is not particularly easy to find, for the labyrinth of the catacombs of Domitilla[3] is vast and intricate. There is nothing to lead us to suppose that there would be a pagan burial here. The layout of the *cubicula* and the intersecting arrangement of the galleries can be found

Facing: detail of the fresco showing the figure of Psyche.

Below: plan of the mapped areas with the gallery of the Flavians.

in other parts of the catacomb. But as we enter the central gallery, we discover a seemingly endless sequence of painted panels that decorate the walls with a myriad of little niches and sections that are veined with red and green. The cupids and putti clambering over the walls, the dolphins darting through the water, and the merry birds all endow these underground skies and seas with a serene as well as joyful dimension.

Up to this point nothing seems to refer to the Christians or their themes, but in the lower wall, not far from the entrance, we see, depicted impressionistically in rapidly applied colors, a Daniel, arms outstretched in the attitude of prayer, between two lions and a dove that is flying towards Noah's ark.

A closer look reveals that this is painted on a superimposed layer of plaster, suggesting that it was a later addition. Furthermore, although the themes painted on the vault can be described as thematically mixed, or rather of a non-specific symbolic type adaptable for pagan or Christian use, the same cannot be said of the paintings on the wall of the second niche, the significance of which leaves no room for doubt. There is none of the simple naturalism, the depiction of an idyllic and sacred dimension, sweet delight or otherworldly beatitude seen elsewhere. Instead we have a clearly designed sequence of landscaped scenes with Priapus as the protagonist.

This god of fertility and virility stands with his enormous phallus among the Christian martyrs and their *loculi* and burial places. If it were not for the fact that he is placed in an out-of-the-way position, inside a single niche, the appearance of his image would seem insulting. The other niches contain more conventional scenes conveying an agrarian and pastoral vision of nature. Here, however, the theme seems to be incontrovertibly

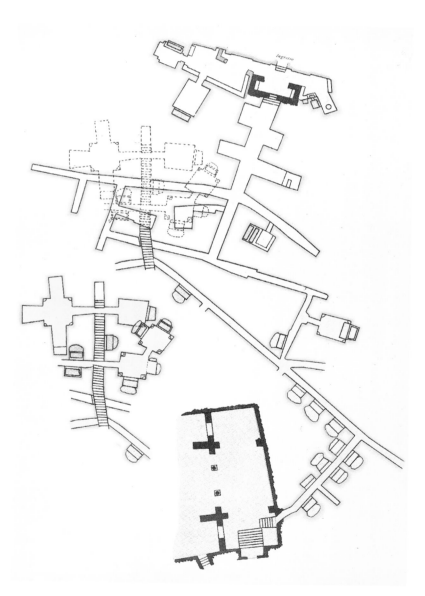

pagan and somewhat inappropriate. It is probable that the hypogeum was originally pagan and that it was only at a later date that it was adapted to the Christian religion, with the creation of loculi and the addition of paintings with more obviously significant themes[4].

We leave by what was originally the entrance, reaching the small square in front of it. The projecting part added on as a vestibule has been divided into several spaces. When, at around the end of the third century AD, the hypogeum had become an integral part of the catacomb cemetery, the room to the right of the entrance was created for funerary banquets, today only the masonry benches that ran along the walls survive. Here, on days commemorating the dead, *Parentalia* or *Feralia*, the *refrigeria* in honor of the deceased were celebrated, with their wealth of ritual and convivial ceremonies. To the left of the entrance, the well and the plumbing arrangements that ensured a supply of water are visible.

On the right, after the banqueting room, we find a small *cubiculum* that preserves, despite the opening up of a number of *loculi*, the remains of a fresco showing the story of Eros and Psyche.

A graceful and smiling Psyche with butterfly wings is shown with Eros in the tranquillity of the Elysian Fields, gathering flowers. It is a delicate depiction, tender in its touch, which does not disturb the sweet tranquillity of the *cubiculum* or the presence of those little children of antiquity who are buried here.

INSULAE, DOMUS

Almost certainly as a result of overcrowding, housing in Rome had developed upwards rather than horizontally. This led to a density of building that, in contrast to the ample spaces granted to the forums, temples, public gardens and many other types of building, gave imperial Rome an appearance more like one of the cities of the East than a geometrical and rationally laid-out *castrum*. The *Regionary Catalogues* list the presence in imperial times of 46,602 *insulae* as opposed to 1,797 *domus*. With one *domus* for every 26 *insulae* it is easy to get some idea of the intense urban development of the city.

It was a city that grew, untidy and unplanned, around dark and narrow lanes, reaching upwards, with buildings that must have looked not so very different from our present-day apartment blocks. "The majesty of the city of Rome, and the considerable increase in its

population led to a need to expand its provision of dwelling houses. The situation itself prompted the attempted solution of building upwards"[1]. The result was living conditions that were very different from the spacious comforts of the *domus*, with their unvarying layout of *fauces, alae, triclinium, tablinum* and *peristylium*[2].

In Rome these two contrasting types of dwelling coexisted, although with a much greater number of the former than the latter. The more modest verticality of one and the aristocratic horizontal development of the other indicated the economic and social condition of the inhabitant. In either case, living in *insulae* or *domus* was expensive. The average rent of even a modest apartment was markedly higher than that paid by people living in the provincial towns.

"The hard-up citizens of Rome ought to have moved away en masse a long time ago. For here it is very difficult for the virtues of those faced with a shortage of money to shine through: all their efforts in Rome are too great! A miserable apartment costs a small fortune, as does keeping servants or allowing oneself the most modest of suppers"[3].

The Aracoeli *insula*

Hidden away in a corner at the foot of the Capitoline Hill, a solid block of ancient brickwork, its sober exterior only slightly relieved by the addition of a small and delicate Romanesque campanile, speaks to us of the everyday life of antiquity. It tells us of the voices and hubbub of "another" Rome, made up, not of monumental piazzas, nymphaea, statues and columns, but of narrow lanes and overcrowded houses.

Squeezed in below the oppressive grandeur of the two staircases of the Aracoeli and the Campidoglio, the *insula* does little to attract the attention or hold the interest of passing visitors. And yet it is one of the few examples in Rome of an ordinary block of houses to have survived from antiquity. It is well preserved and, in addition to the *tabernae* floor (with its mezzanine), has three other existing stories and traces of a fourth.

The *insula* was built in the fourth century BC, in response to the need to house a constantly expanding population. With a ground plan similar to that of a modern apartment building, it consisted of a number of subdivisions into *cenacula*. These were separate dwellings, very similar to those we know today, available for rent.

By contrast, the *domus* – a residence confined to the wealthier classes – developed outwards around a courtyard, consisted of a number of different elements including the *atrium*, the *triclinium*, and the *tablinium*, each with its predetermined function.

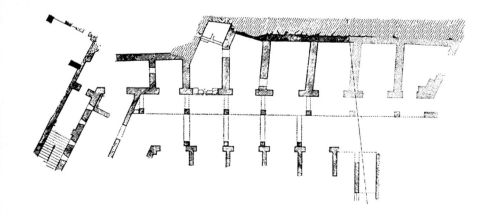

A closer look at the construction of an *insula* shows that the ground floor, when not taken up by a single *domus*, was divided up into a series of *tabernae* (stores or workshops) intended to be both the workplace and private dwelling of the tenant. He and his family lived in these small and dimly lit rooms. A narrow intermediate floor (a kind of mezzanine created within the workshop), lit only by the window at the front of the workshop, was the "night space," where the family slept.

The upper floors were reserved for a number of separate apartments, the size of which diminished as they went up to the top floor, where the room spaces were impossibly small. The facades of these buildings – surprisingly similar to those we know today – had balconies decorated with flowers, porticoes and loggias and presented a pleasing appearance. The interiors, on the other hand, indicate a life of considerable inconvenience, with dubious standards of hygiene.

Transporting ourselves into the past, it is not difficult to imagine these ruins when they were full of noisy and animated life, with faces at the windows calling down, or shouting from the streets below; and an infernal crush of people with, as Juvenal writes, "carts going up and down [...] and flocks stopping in the road and making a din that would waken Drusus or a sea monster." No one seems to have had any thought for the poor occupants packed into the dark and dilapidated rooms of the upper floors.

Juvenal sets the scene for us: "the third floor is on fire and you know nothing about it. From the ground floor up there is confusion, but the last to be roasted alive will be the poor soul who is protected from the rain only by the tiles, where the amorous doves come to lay their eggs."

Above and facing: the rooms on the first floor are in opus reticulatum. *These rooms were larger and more comfortable than those on the floors above, which were intended for poorer people living in appallingly overcrowded conditions.*

The Roman house beneath the Barracco Museum

Facing: view of the portico with its row of smooth polished columns.

Below: plan of the Roman house showing the different phases of building.

In the Via dei Baullari – a street which gives its name of the makers and sellers of trunks (*bauli*) – in the Parione district, there stands a small building of harmonious and restrained design in the best Florentine Renaissance tradition. It was commissioned by Tommaso Le Roy (1523), an important prelate in the papal court, to be his private house, and it was designed in the style then fashionable[1].

The little Baullari palazzo, embellished with elaborate sixteenth-century decoration, stands on the antique ruins of the Campus Martius. We do not know the

One of the columns from the portico showing the reuse of an inverted Doric capital as a base.

name of its architect[2], but beneath the compact elegance of the rusticated stonework and the delicate serlianas, the building stands guard over a small but priceless collection of antiquities, consisting of unique and rare pieces that reveal the refined taste of their tireless collector, Baron Giovanni Barracco.

Egyptian, Assyrian, Etruscan, Greek, and Roman works of art adorn the rooms, offering the opportunity to compare and weigh up the influences and different styles of the most ancient civilizations of

the Mediterranean. In such an important collection, even the basement is not without interest, for it contains the remains of a building from the late imperial period[3]. It is reached by a broad stairway that descends some 5 m., down to the remains of a building of unknown use that opens onto a portico, with a cornice and six polished columns[4].

A cladding of *opera vittata*[5] with courses of brickwork running through it surrounds the row of columns and marks out the extent of the courtyard. Against it stands a marble *labrum*[6] with a hole in the base indicating that it was a fountain. A rich and variegated marble pavement, over a number of different levels[7], covers the floor and contributes to the luxuriousness of the decoration. With both green-veined *cipollino* (Carystian stone) and *opus sectile*[8] in polychrome geometric patterns, this rich pavement indicates a function (whether public or private) of some importance. In any case, the attractiveness of the marble decoration of the walls and the surviving frescoes leave no room for doubt about the splendor of the original decoration. There are little scenes against a painted background depicting playful cupids occupied in various activities such as fishing and hunting; and a multicolored duck with a snake in its beak, all shown in a landscape of lakes and rivers. Unfettered by any concern with content, the scenes confine themselves to a free but detailed naturalism[9].

One might think that this building was a rich patrician *domus* from late antiquity, one of many that occupied the western part of the Campus Martius, were it not for the presence of a bench with measures[10] that seems to indicate use of a public nature. A misreading of one of the frescoes[11] has led to the suggestion that this was a *statio* (a barracks with living quarters) for one of the teams that competed in the circus, the "Prasina" or "Greens," though this may well have been in Vicolo del Pavone. It is more likely that this was a shop intended to serve one of the most populous areas of the city.

Left: one of the surviving frescoes from the interior decoration of the building, showing a multicolored duck with a snake in its beak in a watery landscape.

Below: view of the portico showing the marble labrum *that was used as a fountain.*

The constructions beneath S. Paolo alla Regola

Right: section and plan of the Roman building.

Facing: a view of the underground complex, giving an idea of the typical arrangement in a district of modest houses with shops and storehouses. A glimpse of the reality of the lives of the lower classes of artisans, laborers and tradesmen.

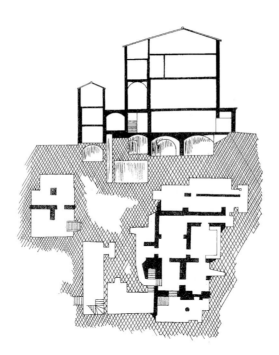

The sixteenth-century walls of a group of houses in the Regola district conceal the traces of a building which can be dated much earlier. A closer look reveals small fragments of Roman masonry visible amongst the later fabric, indicating the presence of a reused building from a very distant past[1].

These clues are an invitation to go through the entrance and step through the little door at the back. Descending the stairway, we are struck by the warm and evocative texture of the brickwork, by the maze of small rooms, and the succession of different spaces and levels. On the lowest level[2], two barrel-vaulted rooms of similar size – once looking onto a street running parallel with the river – appear to date from the Flavian period. They are evidence, albeit scant, of the great food store set up during the period of Domitian. This consisted of a series of warehouses stacked up on top of each other over two floors, known as the *Horrea Vespasiani*.

Remounting the stairs, we find ourselves in a space almost entirely blocked by a massive brick column. All around, the walls reveal traces of houses. It is possible to make out windows, niches for oil-lamps, and stairs, suggesting that this must have been one of the city's many courtyards[3]. It is possible to imagine it as it was, rekindled into vibrant life, with its ancient inhabitants clothing this fragment of a street with the essence of everyday reality.

There are no colored marbles here, no columns or statues, but only modest houses for the common people. A dimension less familiar to us, these buildings nonetheless convey the simple, and in some ways rudimentary, reality of a community of artisans, laborers and tradesmen. Nearby, on the upper story of the *Horrea Vespasiani*, we find modest rooms with black and white mosaics in simple geometric designs. It is even possible to see the fired clay water pipes, reminding us of the ordinary daily life of these ancient people.

Further on, behind two storerooms of the Servian period, there is another interesting courtyard on a much larger scale[4]. Here, wide stretches of plaster work remain, painted to resemble a multicolored marble facing. Traces indicating that this was a fuller's workshop (*fullonica*)[5] have been found, together with some interesting medieval objects: piles of amphorae, shells (*spondylus*) and pigs' teeth. Clearly the presence in the district during the Middle Ages and Renaissance of a number of guilds, such as that of the tanners[6] – concerned with pig flesh – and the *calderari* (from the Latin *caccabarii*) – who made pots and pans – reflects a pattern dating from Roman times, and demonstrates the economic and social continuity to be found in this area of Rome which had direct contact with the river.

Facing: above the stores, on the upper floors of the complex, the rooms have interesting mosaic pavements, indicating that these were living quarters.

Below: fragments of mosaic that once decorated the pavements on the first floor of the building.

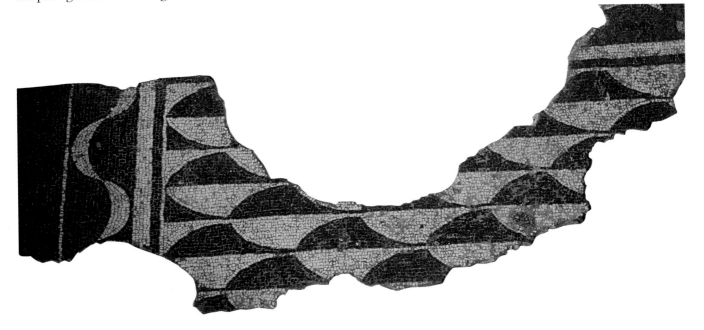

The *Domus Aurea*

Following pages: statue of
Laocôn, *found in 1506
near the* Domus Aurea.

*Facing: detail of the
painted decoration in one
of the rooms. The richness
of the decorative schemes,
the delicate and fluid
touch, combine to create
what can be identified as a
style in its own right – the
so-called Fourth Style.
The sources refer to the*
floridus et humidus *brush
of the painter Fabullus.*

Nero stated that he wanted a house worthy of a sovereign, or rather, "of a man"[1], but his interpretation of these words was based on a highly personal scale of values. It resulted in an imposing and grandiose dwelling that extended into the very heart of the city, almost swallowing it up. This aroused plenty of anger and protest but Nero seems to have ignored all criticism, being less concerned with consensus than with emulating the grandeur of the Hellenistic princes to the east. "Rome will become his house: emigrate to Veio or Quiriti, unless his house takes over Veio as well!"[2].

Vanity and a theocratic view of the Empire had encouraged the emperor to requisition vast areas of the city and to conceive his extraordinary project for a city in the form of a villa. The *magistri* and *machinatores* of this daring plan were the architects Serverus and Celer, who were given the task of translating into architectural form the vision of a *domus* both sumptuous and sacred. They created a residence that was perfectly oriented to the points of the compass, on a hitherto unheard-of scale, arranged around enormous parks and artificial lakes, between the Esquiline, Palatine and Celian Hills, the extremities stretching as far as the Velia. They furnished it with amazing technical devices and rich and precious decorations: "a colossal statue of Nero, 120 feet high, could fit into the vestibule of the house, whose dimensions were such that they allowed space for three mile-long porticoes, and a lake – or, rather, almost a sea – surrounded by buildings as big as cities. Behind were villas with fields, vines and pastures, woods sheltering every kind of domestic and wild animal. Elsewhere, everything was covered in gold, adorned with gems and shells. The banqueting halls had ceilings covered with detachable sheets of ivory, pierced so as to allow showers of flowers and perfumes to fall down. The most important of these halls was circular, and it rotated continually, day and night, like

the earth. The baths were fed by salt and sulfurous waters. When Nero formally opened the building when work was completed, he declared that he was satisfied and said that at last he was going to live in a house worthy of a man"[3].

The site of the vestibule was near the temple of Roma and Venus, in front of the Coliseum, not yet built at that time. The depression where the Coliseum now stands was then occupied by an enormous artificial lake. Other buildings with porticoes, gardens and open countryside surrounded the complex, providing a picturesque framework.

Very little of all this remains today. Only the dark and maze-like rooms of the pavilion on the Oppian Hill survive as testimony to its once immense extent. In the neglected dampness of these rooms it is hard to see why this complex was given the name *Domus Aurea*, the "Golden House." The maze of rooms, arranged in the simplest and most symmetrical manner along the western side, lies around a large rectangular courtyard. On the eastern side the arrangement is rather more complicated, and is concentrated around a large polygonal bay, with the addition of an area radiating out from an octagonal hall.

It is easy to lose one's sense of direction among the interminable succession of spaces and rooms, where cryptoporticus, nymphaea and cubicula can just be made out. We catch glimpses of the astonishing repertoire of that style of fantastic decoration that from the sixteenth century

_____

Insulae, domus

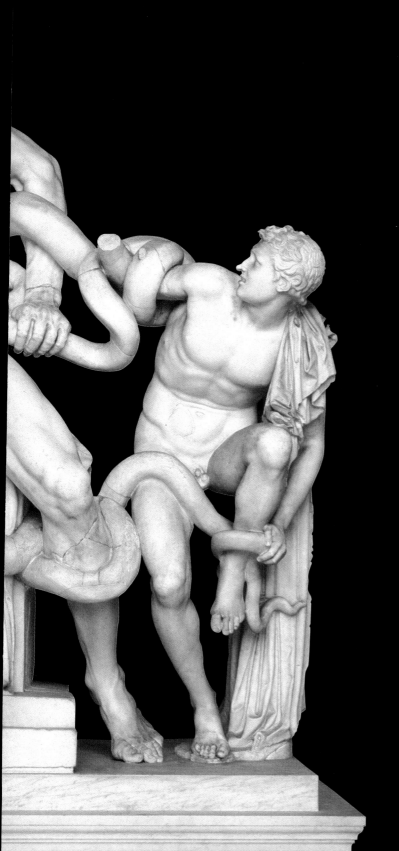

came to be known as "grotesque." It is possible to detect here the brush, or rather the *floridus et humidus*[4] style, of Fabullus, whose rich decorative schemes, soft and fluid touch, and theatrical and fantastical creations are superb examples of the Fourth Style. From the gilded ceiling to the octagonal room, we are dazzled by the interplay of colors and his fantastic imagination. We can only imagine the original effect of this decor: the dazzling luminosity, bathed in sunlight; the colors, the gold of the walls, the precious materials. Inevitably, we call to mind the philosophical principles that inspired a sovereign who aspired to the crown of the Sun god, influenced no doubt by a culture permeated with Mazdaism and Mithraism, which focused on sun worship. Suddenly everything seems to fit into place: there is a logic, however egocentric and eccentric, in the calculated orientation of the rooms, in the scenic effects, in the gilded ceilings. The presence of the colossus in the entrance vestibule, dressed as Helios, but with the features of the emperor, seems to conform to these principles, and to the idea of an imperial residence as an *instrumentum regni*. The policy follows a very eastern model of the sacred image of the sovereign, designed to celebrate the divinity of the prince. Nero's identification with the sun sanctioned a fruitful and prolific identification of the one with the other, for a universal government of the kingdom, as for the cosmos.

FUNCTION AND DELIGHT

Although in the preceding chapters it has been possible to group buildings according to their similarity of use, such a categorization is not easy in the descriptions that follow here. This section brings together buildings with different uses, but which can be grouped under the general heading of public buildings, or rather, buildings for public use. A range of buildings are included which, although very different, nevertheless fall within this category of "public architecture."

Latrines and cisterns, for example, provide evidence of the high level of hydraulic engineering existing at the time, as well as the intelligent use of water, managed by specially selected and highly specialized functionaries, the *curatores aquarum*. A sundial, on the other hand, appears more as an object with a symbolic value or as a vehicle for propaganda. Yet its function as an instrument for measuring time is important. Similarly, the stadium was both a medium for celebration and an instrument for popular consensus, proving the efficacy of the policy of *panem et circenses*. Prisons fulfill a function that is no less useful and acceptable. The Mamertine prison, because of its strategic position, can be seen as the most representative and the grimmest of them.

Thus there is a wide variety of public buildings which respond to the twin demands of function and delight. They provide us with a picture of Rome in the centuries of the Empire, illustrating both its squalor and its splendor.

The "*Sette Sale*"

Previous pages: one of the passageways in the Stadium of Domitian.

Right: view of the front of the imposing "Seven Halls" cistern. One of the largest cisterns in antiquity, its perfect and efficient system supplied water to the first great bath complex in Rome, the Baths of Trajan.

Among the hidden treasures of the Oppian Hill is one of the largest and most imposing cisterns to survive from antiquity: the *"Sette Sale"* ("Seven Halls"). Proud and severe, spreading towards the street like the jaws of a great whale, it reminds us of the ancient pride of the architectural genius of the Romans, illustrating as it does the Vitruvian principle of "solidity, utility and beauty." Pliny the Elder contrasted "the useless and mad ostentation of the Pyramids" with the proud Roman principle of constructing buildings that were both necessary and beautiful, and that were above all solid and long-lasting. The monumentality of Rome was an expression of the sentiment of the ethical and political greatness of an Empire conscious of its historical mission and its universal role.

The reservoir was always much visited and explored: Stendhal included it in his description of walks around Rome. He visited the long dark galleries, covered with climbing plants, in December 1828.

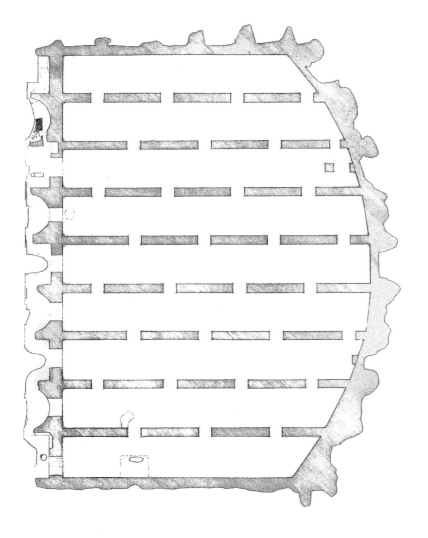

Above: plan of the cistern.

Facing: view of the series of openings connecting the different halls. Each gallery communicates with the others by means of varying axes, so as to offer greater resistance to the pressure of the water that flowed from one to the next, thus avoiding the setting up of currents.

under the earth, the galleries extended away from the eyes of the observer into an endless perspective of rows of doors.

Such a well-devised complex, so vast but so functional, was needed to create the best possible arrangement for a reservoir with a capacity of 8,165,000 liters of water, fed by a branch of one of the aqueducts carrying water into Rome by way of the Porta Maggiore and the Esquiline Hill, probably the Aqua Julia. It was a perfect and highly effective mechanism for the supply of water to the first of the great baths in Rome: the Baths of Trajan, built by the architect Apollodorus of Damascus who was famed for the inventiveness and ingenuity of his designs. The nymphaea, fountains and pools of the baths were brought to life by the impressive flow of this supply of water that was to run constantly until the devastation wreaked by Vitigis cut it off.

Deeply embedded in the ground, the only part of this imposing cistern still visible is the attractive facade on two stories, with a fine outer wall in brick. The facade is enlivened by nine niches[1], alternately semicircular and rectangular, corresponding to the same number of rooms. Within the niches on the lower story, it is possible to see at the top of the *fistulae*[2] holes, placed one on either side of the opening of the rectangular niches, and centrally in the semicircular niches. Attached to the opening of each *fistula* was a lead plate nailed to the wall and covered with *opus signinum* to prevent the water leaking through.

As he groped his way through the dense forest of rooms and corridors, between the damps walls still coated with mud and slime, he was able to discover how nothing had been left to chance. Every element, down to the smallest detail, spoke of the skilled mastery of the techniques of antiquity: the calculated alignment of the halls, the cladding of *opus signinum*, the absence of dead ends. Here,

A steep iron stairway marks the start of this fascinating underground journey, unique in its arrangement and sequence of spaces and openings. Once inside, nine long halls[3] lying parallel to each other form a vast space bounded by three straight walls and one, to the far side[4], that is curved. This was to allow the water to run towards the channel, and to avoid dead ends. Each gallery communicates with its neighbor by way of four arches, their openings staggered so as to offer greater resistance to the pressure of the water flowing from one to the other, and to prevent the creation of currents and eddies. The conduit bringing in the water was in the center of the curved back wall. From there the water flowed through the sequence of galleries rendered waterproof by the application of a cladding of *opus signinum*.

The succession of barrel-vaulted halls and the play of light and shade created by the endless rows of openings leaves a memorable impression, so that we forget that the cistern was constructed not as an aesthetic object but in order to avoid the dangers of flooding and currents.

The cistern was used until at least the fifth century AD, and had, on the terrace above, a number of buildings probably related to its function. In later antiquity a rich *domus* was built over them, the remains of which can still be seen. The magnificent mosaic pavements are an indication of the grandeur of this ancient house, which belonged not to the shadows of the world below, but to the light of day.

The Roman cistern in the Via Cristoforo Colombo

The preoccupied drivers going down the Via Colombo can easily fail to notice the huge round cistern taking up one side of the street. For the more attentive observer, this great cylindrical structure of brick epitomizes the link between past and present where an intense relationship with history, so characteristic of the urban fabric of the city, is evident.

Although surrounded and hemmed in by apartment blocks and high-rise buildings, this monument to civil engineering still asserts the spirit of the Romans and their skill in constructing buildings at once solid, useful and dignified, capable of withstanding the ravages of time. Cisterns, fountains and aqueducts, with their rational structure, were the pride of the Romans, and their answer to the architecture of the Greeks, based essentially on aesthetic principles.

Similar in many respects to other reservoirs from Roman times, the cistern in the Via Colombo must once have been partially buried, or entirely below ground. The fact that it now partially protrudes from the ground is due to the brutal roadworks carried out in the street, once called the Via Imperiale, now renamed the Via Colombo. This intervention was infamous for the devastation caused to the surrounding area and the ancient buildings, and it led to the diversion underground of the river Almone and the demolition of all the existing structures running along its banks.

The consistent lowering of the ground level since antiquity caused the cistern to emerge on the surface from beneath a block, built above the redundant reservoir, that was being demolished. Excavations led to the cistern's gradual uncovering.

Two vast cylindrical constructions were discovered, the largest of which was identified as a cistern, with a spacious circular outer shell containing concentric rings built of *opus reticulatum*, dating from the second decade of the second century AD. The first ring consists of ten radiating spaces, connected by arched

openings. The inner ring has a roof subdivided into five-arched bays. This unique internal arrangement creates a regular and attractive rhythm.

An iron stairway leads down into the interior[1], and first into a sort of vestibule[2], barrel vaulted and trapezoid in plan, with areas covered in *opus signinum*. From here

a seemingly endless sequence of bays opens out[3], drawing the eye along the curving perspectives of the halls to admire the architectural and imaginative skill of the designer. The bays and inner ring are linked by arches and openings that connect the halls into an intricate labyrinth of spaces, confusing the visitor with its

External view of the wall of the drum of the cistern faced in opus reticulatum *(second century AD). Very similar to other Roman reservoirs, this one in the Via Colombo must have been partly or completely buried underground.*

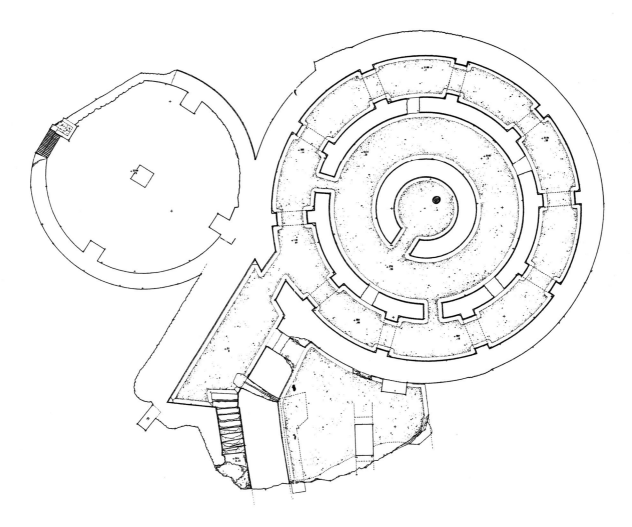

Facing: view of the curved innermost corridor, with a vault divided into bays with five arches. This arrangement, combined with that of the outer ring, generates a regular and lively rhythm.

endless curving rhythm. In this fascinating context of curving surfaces, the technical details relating to stylistic sources, waterproofing, and the construction of the vaults could pass almost unnoticed. And yet this is a highly skilled piece of engineering, as can be seen from the remarkable efficiency of the construction, the waterproof cladding of *opus signinum*, as well as the presence of rounded moldings provided to avoid sharp-edged corners.

Rather than supplying a villa (for which there is no evidence), as might have been expected, the cistern must have provided water for the fields of an estate, by means of an aqueduct. The site lies in what was suburban Rome and the area is characterized by the presence of tombs, funerary monuments, villas and large agricultural plots. The fortuitous discovery of this great reservoir provides evidence of the splendid buildings of another age, and leaves us with a dignified and eloquent fragment to stand against the modern high-rise buildings nearby.

The Augustan sundial (Horologium Augusti)

Today the obelisk of Psammetichus II (early sixth century BC) stands proud and solemn before the Chamber of Deputies, casting its slim shadow across the Piazza di Montecitorio. It was brought from Heliopolis and was placed by Augustus in the Campus Martius to serve as the pointer, or gnomon, for his majestic sundial. At 21.8 m. in height, its pointed top directed towards the Sun[1], it commemorated the conquest of Egypt. Like a ray of solidified light, it casts its shadow over a vast travertine base forming the dial or face. It indicated the hours, days, cycle of seasons, winds and astral influences by means of markers set into the dazzling white stone. As a symbol of the cosmos it recorded the time and seasons in honor of the emperor. "The divine Augustus attributed miraculous powers to the obelisk that stands in the Campus Martius, believing that it could capture the shadow of the sun and determine the length of the days and nights. Thus he had made a pavement of slabs of a size proportionate to the height of the obelisk, so that the shadow was equal to this paved area at the sixth hour (which is to say, at midday) of the winter solstice. Little by little, day by day, this would shrink and grow again, indicated by bronze rulers inserted in the pavement. It should be known that this was the work of the astronomer Novius Facundus. The latter added a gilded globe to the top of the obelisk, thus allowing the shadow to gather at the summit, and preventing the apex from casting too long a shadow: it is said that in doing this he was inspired by the human head"[2].

For the construction of this clock (in 10 BC), famous astronomers and mathematicians from Alexandria were sent for, men whose erudition enabled them to harness time within a schematic grid marked out on the surface of the pavement by a clear sequence of bronze scales, creating an immense quadrant whose metal strips provided a geometric, solar and sacred function. It was not just an instrument for measuring, but rather a monument to the sun and to the stars, and to the *aurea aetas* of Augustus. On September 23, Augustus' anniversary and also the day of the fall equinox, the pointed shadow of the

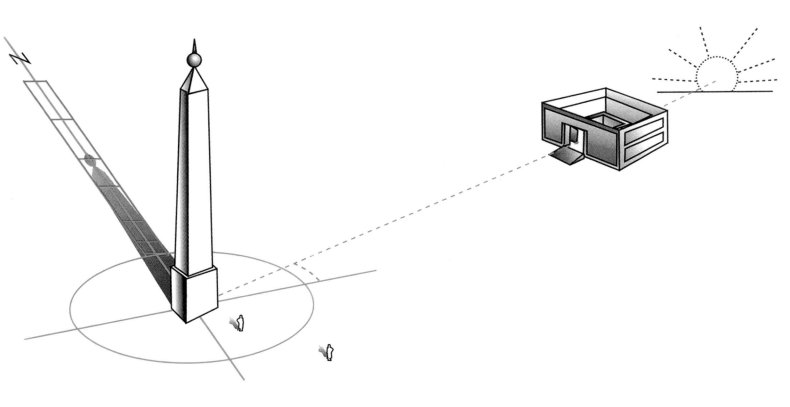

gnomon stretched out towards the center of the Ara Pacis (Altar of Peace), with a clearly theatrical and commemorative effect. It was a way of marking symbolically the divine origins of the emperor, signaled out by destiny to introduce a new era of peace and greatness for the city of Rome and its empire. The obelisk, of pink granite, was, furthermore, set up in such a way that one of its sides faced the rising sun on April 21, the date of the foundation of Rome. Thus everything was carefully arranged so as to emphasize the divine destiny of the birth of the man who was the first to assume the title of "Augustus," a destiny decreed in the stars and sanctioned by the sun.

Of this emphatic and celebrative piazza nothing remains today (once 160 m. long from east to west and 75 m. from north to south)[3]. Of that desire to register the hours only a minute fragment remains, a marble fragment with the bronze markers still embedded in it, recovered 8 m. down in a cellar at 48 Via del Campo di Marzio[4]. Passing through a courtyard, this under-

ground cavity can only be reached by means of a ladder, but the effort involved is worthwhile. Set in the stone between the signs of Virgo and Aries, a Greek inscription can be read: "Trade winds weaken" (*Etesiai Pauontai*). The assertion in the words seems almost an imperative that carries us to distant places, to the eastern Mediterranean where those fierce winds still blow today.

Above and following pages: the Augustan Ara Pacis (Altar of Peace).

Function and delight

The Stadium of Domitian

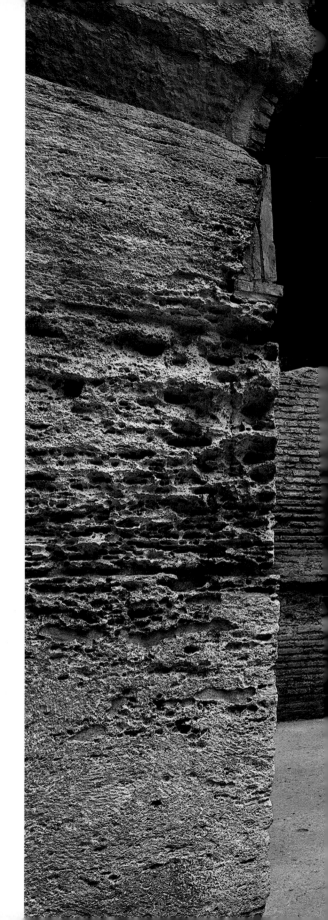

View of the walls supporting the stepped seats of the ancient cavea of the stadium. A complete section is preserved intact near one of the main entrances.

If we ignore the sound of the water gushing from Bernini's fountains, we can still sense in the Piazza Navona the ancient atmosphere of the games held there in honor of Jupiter Capitolinus. Indeed, "Navona," derived from *agone* meaning athletic games, preserves the memory of the original function of the place as a stadium, as do the rounded ends of the piazza. It is easy to imagine the excitement of the spectators, shouting and betting; the hubbub, and the attempts of traders and prostitutes to attract custom.

Constructed under Domitian in 86 AD, the stadium was intended to hold games following the Greek model. Thus Rome had its *Certamen Capitolinus*, a collection of competitions held every five years and which included, along with the sporting events, competitions of a more literary type. The series of events aimed at a mixture of activities, so that a running race[1] and a demonstration of eloquence might be followed by boxing and Latin poetry, javelin throwing and Greek poetry,

in a competitive succession combining the athletic disciplines and the arts. The Agon, as conceived by Domitian, was marked in the program of the capital's festivals as an elaborate occasion, opening with a ceremony in the presence of the emperor who, for the occasion, "appeared shod in sandals, wearing a purple toga in the Greek style and a golden crown recalling the depictions of Jupiter, Juno and Minerva, while seated around him were the Flamen Dialis and the priest of the Flavians, similarly dressed, except that their crowns bore the portrait of the emperor"[2].

In order to accommodate the many elements of these games there was not only the stadium (*circus agonalis*)[3], but also an *odeon* for musical performances,

recitations and poetry competitions. Both these structures survive within the fabric of the modern city that still proudly preserves its ancient plan. The Piazza Navona stands over the flat part of the stadium, while the nearby Palazzo Massimo alle Colonne, designed by Peruzzi, follows the original theater-shaped plan of the *odeon*. Going by the numbers involved – the odeon had places for about 10,000 spectators, and the stadium 30,000 – the public had a strong appetite for this type of spectacle. Nevertheless, these numbers were small in comparison with the crowds of people who flocked to the amphitheaters (the Coliseum alone could hold 80,000). This was not only due to the difference in

Function and delight

popular appeal between the *munera* (gladiatorial combat) and races and speech-making competitions; it also reflected a certain degree of moralizing chauvinism, in that the athletic competitions were "imported" and, furthermore, the competing athletes were naked. The Greek-style contests of the *Agon Capitolinus* were not approved of by the Romans, not even by the intellectuals who equally rejected gladiatorial combat, calling it bloody and brutal. Cicero approvingly recalled the words of Ennius, according to whom "scandal begins when a man reveals his naked body before his fellow citizens"[4]. Tacitus takes up the same theme, writing: "the only thing lacking was for them to show themselves naked, taking up the fighter's *cestus* and thinking only of these combats instead of military service"[5]. The final shot is launched by Seneca: "How feeble of soul are those whose muscles and shoulders we admire"[6].

The circus was about 275 m. long and 106 m. wide, with one straight end to the south and one curved end to the north. It had a severe and imposing appearance, with its line of columns and arcades[7] sheltering a range of establishments from shops to brothels. The construction of the exterior involved two orders of arches on travertine piers[8], alternating with statues and other decorations, giving it a dignified and monumental appearance. From a balcony in the Piazza Tor Sanguigna it is possible to look out over the stadium and visualize its original dimensions due to

the survival of one of the main entrances[9] with its beautiful travertine arcade and what is left of the prothyrum (entrance passageway) standing before it, with one remaining broken column in *portasanta*. It is possible to descend some 3.5 m. below ground, where enough of a complete section of the ancient cavea of the stadium remains[10] to allow us to form an idea of the structure.

Above: general view of one of the central passages. One of the statues of Apollo Lyceius of the Praxiteles school discovered here can be seen in the middle.

Facing: the rhythmical arrangement of passages and succession of rooms allows us to appreciate the fine brick internal masonry.

A latrine in the Via Garibaldi

The painted paneling of the latrine (second phase of painting). Delicate polychrome bands divide the walls, against a delicate light background on which delightful little figures can still be discerned.

From the early centuries of the Empire, the Romans had begun to pride themselves on their ability to construct works that were not only beautiful but also useful and ingenious: "The Romans thought above all of those things that they [the Greeks] had neglected: of paving the streets, channeling water, constructing sewers that could empty all the waste of the city into the Tiber [...] thanks to the supplies of water brought by aqueducts, sufficient to allow rivers

to run through the city and along sub-terranean conduits"[1].

In fact, the sewers of Rome had never been linked up with the dwellings of the *insulae*, and it would be a mistake to imagine that Roman houses in those times benefitted from a system of waste disposal. Apart from the better off – the rich owners of the *domus* – who had their own private latrines, everyone else had to use the public latrines (*foricae*). This meant walking to the nearest *forica* and paying a

Detail of painted plaster from the earlier phase, showing an elegant decoration with candelabra, a good indication of the level of refinement that could be found in a public building of this type.

Latrine in the Via Garibaldi **259**

small sum of money. The communal latrines were administered by the *conductores foricarum*, specially contracted officials appointed by the authorities.

These latrines were, for the most part, attractive places, richly ornamented, where people often came to meet and gossip, or even obtain an invitation to a meal: "In every latrine / now going to one, now another, / Vacerra passes his hours and sits all day. / His great need is to eat, not to crap"[2]. There was comfortable seating along the benches, or even on seats sculpted to resemble dolphins, surrounded by sumptuous mosaic or painted decorations, richly ornamented with statues, stuccoes and fountains. The comfort of these pleasant and refined places recalls all the opulence of the East.

The lower classes did not, of course, frequent such luxurious places, making do – at best – with pots, thereby assisting some fuller who could easily make use of urine in his trade. Several examples of latrines survive in Rome to this day. One of these was discovered in 1963 when a supporting wall of the square in front of the church of S. Pietro in Montorio collapsed. It is an interesting structure that still retains its rich painted decoration, documenting the organization of a system of public convenience that is as intriguing as it was efficient. It is still possible to see the drain that carried away the waste.

The absence of any trace of brackets on the walls indicates that the cladding was of wood. Two areas of painted plaster remain on the walls, combining in an attractive decorative effect. The place would almost seem to be a kind of small reception room, were it not for the very prominent inscriptions and graffiti on the walls reminding us that this ancient building, now a document of the past, was once home to the lewd and obscene atmosphere of the urinal and public latrine.

Facing: fragment of a mosaic pavement of black and white tesserae.

Below: scratched into the plaster of the walls are a number of graffiti, drawings, marks and inscriptions that remind us that, despite the elegant decoration, this place must still have had something of the lewd and obscene atmosphere of the public urinal and latrine.

The VII cohort of guards

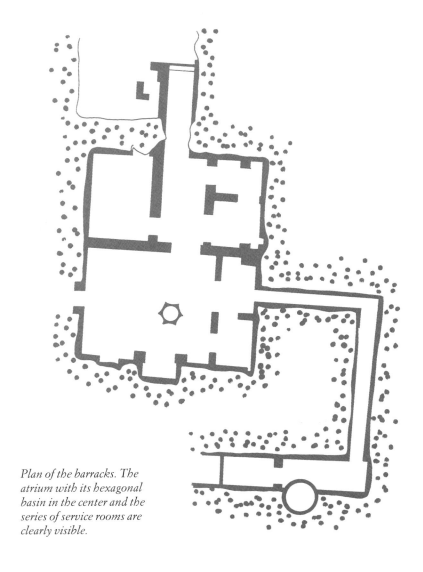

Plan of the barracks. The atrium with its hexagonal basin in the center and the series of service rooms are clearly visible.

Contrasting with the magnificence of Rome's spectacular forums, great temples, equestrian bronze statues, brilliantly colored marbles, vast squares enclosed by colonnades, statues and fountains; the Rome of grand occasions and the rhetoric of public spaces, was another Rome, in the minor key, built of brick and wood, squeezed into small spaces, narrow lanes, and crushed in between the overcrowded houses. This "other" modest city was the city of the ordinary, working population, and must have been very similar to certain quarters of modern Marrakech. It had developed as a result of unplanned urban expansion, the houses crowding together in those spaces not swallowed up by the overbearing imperial dwellings and the grandeur of the great squares. Life in this other Rome was very different from the glittering life that was led in the aristocratic villas with their porticoes and gardens, their precious furnishings; the vast scale and "horizontal" direction of

their development combined with the solidity and quality of their fabric.

The other side of the coin reveals a more untidy and unassuming picture, with *insulae* that developed "vertically," to a height of five or six stories, made of poor and non-durable materials. Height was often gained at the expense of solidity, and collapses were the order of the day. Juvenal writes: "In Preneste, with its cool breezes, in Bolsena, standing amid the wooded hills, or in peaceful Gabi, or on the eroded hill at Tivoli, who is ever afraid that his house might collapse around him? We, instead, insist on living in a city held up for the most part by insecure beams, because the administrator knows of no other solution to hold up the walls, and

when he had blocked up the gaps of an old crack, he tells us to sleep peacefully with this constant threat over our heads"[1]. The almost universal use of wood for ceilings and room partitions, as well as for the fittings and furniture, represented a constant threat to the survival of the house and its tenants. The passageways, supposedly acting as fire-breaks, were almost useless in the face of the constant use within the houses of portable stoves, candles, lamps and torches. "Ucalegon cries out for them to bring water while trying to save his few poor belongings: beneath his feet the third floor is already in flames"[2]. In fact, water was in very short supply in these houses, and generally restricted, in exchange for a fee, to those wealthy enough to live on the ground floor. It would have been wiser to follow the advice given by Juvenal: "Far better to live where there are never fires and one can sleep at night without being in constant fear"[3].

In 6 AD Augustus set up a properly constituted military body, the new militia of the *vigiles*. It was their task not only to deal with fires, but also to provide a night-time patrol against burglars, thieves and receivers of stolen goods. This body, overseen by a *praefectus vigilum*[4], was organized into seven cohorts, divided in turn into seven centuries[5]. Taking account of Augustus' subdivision of the city into 14 districts (*regiones*), each cohort was responsible for two districts, one containing their headquarters (*statio*), the other a garrison with a body of guards (*excubitorium*).

The only surviving building is the smaller garrison of the permanent detachment of the VII cohort, which was responsible for order in the "XIV Region" (Trastevere). This subterranean building[6] was constructed at the end of the second century AD, over a private house.

A broad stairway leads to the interior, opening into a huge hall dimly lit from a few windows placed high up in the walls. The walls, covered with a warm red cladding of brick, betray signs of the ancient moldings and architectural aspirations of a building with a clearly functional use. A large mosaic pavement of black and white tesserae, now destroyed, covered the hall with an aquatic dance of sea-monsters and tritons, chosen to symbolize their mythical triumph over fire. The eight-sided form of a beautiful hexagonal basin interrupted this revolving dance, drawing the eye to the opposite wall with its elegant portal, an intriguing architectural indication of a probable *genius exubitorii*[7]. Next to the main hall are a series of service rooms, one of which seems to have been for bathing. A dense series of graffiti[8] on the plaster records the names of the guards; their fears, their superstitions and, above all, their labours, carried out with few and rudimentary aids: poles, ladders, ropes, and special sheets, called *centomes*, that, when wetted, were used to stifle the flames. The guards had special pumps (*siphones*) to feed water through pipes; otherwise they had to rely on the strength of their arms, passing buckets coated with pitch (*vasa spartea*) or containers known as *hamae* from hand to hand. From the graffiti we learn also of the drudgery and danger of night duty, and the difficulties experienced by the *sebaciarii*[9] in preparing torches for illumination at night, guaranteeing some degree of security to the inhabitants. Juvenal writes: "You can die as many times as there are open windows at night looking onto the street along which you are passing. Just wish, and cling to this miserable hope, that the windows will do nothing worse than tip out the contents of their basins on your head"[10].

Notes

MITHRAISM

[1] For a better understanding of the god Mithra, or Mithras, it is necessary to look at the great legacy of Persian texts (*Avesta*) that set down the reforms of *Zarathushtra* or *Zoroastrer*. This movement of a montheistic character, thanks to a compromise with the older Arian naturism, successfully established itself between the seventh and sixth centuries BC. At the head of the divine hierarchy, it introduced the figure of *Ahura Mazda*, "the wise lord," source of pure and perfect understanding, who oversaw all good creation. To assist him in this work, Ahura was accompanied by six "immortal saints," *Amesha Spenta*, his coeternal manifestations and guarantors with him of justice, truth and purity. Associated with this upper hierarchy of divinities was another made up of subordinate angels; their leader was Mithra, an Arian god who formed part of the Mazdean pantheon. The tenth *Yast* (Canto X) of the *Avesta* was dedicated to him. For further reading on the religious implications of the Persian Mithra and his connections with Roman Mithraism see the Bibliography.

[2] The pirates based in Cilicia, in Asia Minor, numbered some 20,000. At the peak of their power they were active in the entire Mediterranean area.

[3] It gained popularity in the military environment on account of its warrior-like character and its emphasis on redemption.

[4] The life-giving stone has a cosmic value in the context of the mithraic religion (see the following paragraph for a discussion of this). In the mithraic view, the earth (and hence stone) was a symbol of the matter of which the cosmos is made (cf. Porphyrius, note 6). Mithras is seen as a god of light and the Sun represents the light born of the cosmos or, rather, of the solid (material) vault of the heavens.

[5] These were represented symbolically by the trials that the initiate had to overcome in order to earn a place among the ranks of the adepts.

[6] Porphyrius, *De antro nympharum*, 6, 20 (*Liantro delle ninfe*, Adelphi, Milan, 1986).

[7] Porphyrius, *op. cit.*, 5, 1.

[8] Tertullian, *De corona*, 15, 3 (*De corona*, Mondadori, Milan, 1992).

[9] Firmicus Maternus, *De errore profanarum religionum*, 5, 2 (*De errore profanarum religionum*, La Nuova Italia, Florence, 1969).

[10] Cf. Note 6. The astronomy of ancient Rome was based on the Ptolemaic system, according to which the celestial vault (the sky with fixed stars) rotated daily around the earth. Even the sun, along with the other planets, moved around the earth.

[11] Origen, *Contra Celsum*, VI, 22.

[12] Apuleius, *Asinus aureus*, XI, 23, 7 (*Le Metamorfosi o l'Asino d'oro*, Rizzoli, Milan, 1977).

[13] We know of the different stages of mithraic initiation from a text by St. Jerome (*Epistolae ad Laetam*, CVII, 2).

[14] Merkelbach (*Mithras*, Konigstein, 1984) has recently put forward the view that the second degree of initiation – *Nymphus* – meant "male chrysalis," a neologism formed from *nympha* in its meaning of the chrysalis of bees, wasps and butterflies.

[15] We know that the first three degrees constituted a lower level of initiation that did not give admittance to participation in the mysteries and relegated its members to the position of servants. The higher levels, by contrast, raised the members to the rank of "participant."

[16] This association was anything but secure, however, for it is contradicted on numerous occasions. It should be said that in the paintings in the Santa Prisca mithraeum we find a different series: the patron and "guardian" of *Corax* was Mercury, Venus that of *Nymphus*, Mars of *Miles*, Jupiter of *Leo*, the Moon (Luna) of *Perses*, the Sun of *Heliodromus*, and Saturn of *Pater*.

[17] In many mithraea these stages were symbolically represented on the floors or walls (for example in the mithraeum "of the seven spheres" or "seven doors" at Ostia).

[18] Tertullian, *op. cit.*, XV, 4. It was probably with such a ceremony that the *miste* was initiated into the grade of *miles*.

[19] J. Darmesteter, *Le Zend-Avesta*, Paris, 1892. *Haoma* was an intoxicating drink already used in the Mazdean rite, and mentioned with an invocation in the *Yast*. There are 21 of these *Yast*, hymns or songs for use by lay people, dedicated to the Yazata or lower gods of the Mazdean theology, one of whom was Mithra. He was an Arian god who entered the ranks of the Mazdean Yazata in the time of Artaserse II.

[20] Justin, *I Apologia*, LXVI, 4 (*Le due Apologie*, Edizioni Paoline, Rome, 1983).

[21] This is the Anastasi papyrus (*Supplément grec du récueil magique*, n.574) wrongly believed to be a mithraic liturgy. It belongs more properly to the syncretic culture of the Egyptian and Hellenistic-Alexandrine world.

[22] It is not known whether actual sacrifices of bulls took place during the rituals. It is more likely, not least because of the objective difficulties associated with bringing the animal inside, that the act of consuming bread and wine was a symbolic substitute for the event. Nevertheless, there are those who insist that the bloody sacrifice did take place, citing the evidence of such elements as the *fossa sanguinis* at the mithraeum at the Baths of Caracalla. Such a ceremony would have been the genuine *taurobolium* (baptism by bull's blood, of the type practiced by those present at the cult of the *Magna mater*).

[23] Macrobius, *Saturnaliorum libri*, I, 117, 58 (*I Saturnali*, UTET, Turin, 1967).

[24] In Zoroastrianism and Zurvanism, endless time stands at the highest point of the divine hierarchy and is the origin of everything.

[25] Statues of the dadophori, or painted representations of them, can often be found at the entrance to sanctuaries as heralds.

[26] Ostia, with its high density of mithraea (there are at least 18) has deliberately been omitted from this number, since, as a separate town from the city of Rome, it would require a chapter to itself.

[27] The effects must have given rise to trance-like experiences of the kind still found in some of the rituals of the Latin-American Macumba religion.

MITHRAEUM OF THE CIRCUS MAXIMUS

[1] These were the starting boxes for the chariot races.

[2] This reads: *"Deo Soli Invicto Mithrae Ti(berius) Cl(audius) Hermes ob votum dei typum d(ono) d(at)"* ("To the undefeated Sun god Mithras, Tiberius Claudius Hermes following a vow offers the image of the god").

[3] The work can be dated with reasonable certainty to the third century AD.

[4] Pumice stone was used to simulate the appearance of a cave or grotto.

[5] It is possible that the parallel-piped base was an altar.

[6] This niche was created during a second phase. Previously in this spot there had been, in all probability, the great relief showing the *tauroctonia*.

[7] Some scholars read this as: *"Magicas / inhiti fas / ey bene Gentio / Aternius / Biro"* (It is permitted to enter into the magic [arts]. Long live Gentius, Aeternius, Biro). For others, the first three lines should read: *"Magicas / inbictas: cede Degentio* (Yield the undefeated magic arts to Decentius").

[8] It is likely that, given the proximity to the *carceres* of the Circus Maximus, that this was a community with links to chariot racing.

BARBERINI MITHRAEUM

[1] The villa was designed by Gustavo Giovannoni and Marcello Piacentini.

[2] The first phase goes back to the first half of the first century AD, the second to the beginning of the third century AD.

[3] This is the text of the inscription: *Yperanthes basem inbicto donum dedit* (AE 1948, 100).

[4] In depictions of the *tauroctonia*, the iconography almost always shows Mithras with a cloak scattered with stars.

[5] This, as other following scenes, can be found in the fresco in the Marino mithraeum, similar in general iconography to that of the Barberini mithraeum. The story of Jove and the battle with the giants can be read as piece of sycretic borrowing where the cosmic elements, made divine, are fused with the figures of the Greek, Roman and Persian pantheon: the Sky with Jove, Zeus, Ahura Mazda; the Earth with Juno, Hera, Spenta Armaiti; the Ocean with Neptune, Poseidon, Apam-Napat.

[6] In the Persian theology underlying Mithraism, time creates the cosmos over a series of generations. The first couple created by time is the Sky and the Earth. The Earth, impregnated by the Sky, gives birth to the Ocean, the three creating a trinity.

[7] By virtue of his middle position and mediating function, he is given the middle day of the month, the sixteenth.

[8] The last three scenes are connected with the legendary story of the god and his pact with the Sun.

MITHRAEUM OF S. CLEMENTE

[1] It may be a spring or an ancient aqueduct capable of supplying hundreds of liters of water per second.

[2] Porphyrius, *op. cit.*, 5, 5.

MITHRAEUM OF THE BATHS OF CARACALLA

[1] The podiums and piers are later than the walls of the room.

[2] This detail is only found in one other mithraeum in Lazio, at Sutri.

[3] Tertullian, *De baptismo*, V (*De baptismo*, Paravia, Turin, 1968).

DEATH

[1] Hence the name of *Lemuria* for the second festival of the dead that took place on 9, 11 and 13 May. On these occasions the temples remained closed and weddings were forbidden.

[2] Plautus, *Mostellaria*, 490 (*Mostellaria–Persa*, Mondadori, Milan, 1981).

[3] Ovid, *Fastorum libri*, V, 429–444 (*I Fasti*, Zanichelli, Bologna, 1983).

[4] It was essentially the *adprecatio* to the Manes, expressed by the initials D.M. or D.M.S. that was followed by the name of the dedicator and dedicatee with their dates.

[5] Ovid, (*op. cit.*, II, 553–570) gives a detailed account of the *Parentalia* and the connections connected with this festival.

[6] Ausonius, *Epistulae*, XXXI (*Epistole*, Il Cardo, Venice, 1995). A special occasion in this sense was the *Rosalia* that took place in May and June and, while not strictly connected with the deceased, allowed people the opportunity to visit the tombs of relatives and scatter them with roses.

[7] Polybius, *Historiae*, VI, 53 (*Storie*, Mondadori, Milan, 1970).

[8] J. M. C. Toynbee, *Morte e sepoltura nel mondo romano*, L'Erma di Bretschneider, Rome, 1993.

TOMBS ON THE VIA LATINA

[1] The archaeological park of the Via Latina is the result of the independent and passionate research of a private individual, Lorenzo Fortunati, who, in the mid-nineteenth century, after a considerable period of excavation, uncovered a long stretch of the road, complete with its tombs and graves, discovering in addition the remains of a large residential villa and the traces of the basilica of S. Stefano.

[2] This is a frequent style of tomb, designed to look like a two-storied temple over an underground chamber. Discovered here was the so-called Barberini Sarcophagus with the myth of Protesilaus and Laodameia carved on it, now in the Vatican Museums.

[3] The name must be taken as arbitrary, having no historical basis, since no inscriptions were found inside. The tomb can be dated by a brick stamp of 159 AD of the Antonine period, probably between the end of the reign of Antoninus Pius and the beginning of that of Marcus Aurelius.

[4] Here an inscription that mentions the college of the Pancratii was also discovered, hence the name of the tomb.

[5] It is an ark-shaped sarcophagus, without inscription or portrait.

MONTE DEL GRANO

[1] Its particular form resembling an inverted corn measure probably explains both the origin of the name and of the legend.

[2] This can be translated as: "To dig and extract and break all that quantity of existing travertine within and without the mound known as Monte del Grano", and above all "in order to carry it away and transform it into good and convenient lime."

[3] The discovery was made in 1582. Today the sarcophagus is kept in the Capitoline Museums.

[4] Flaminio Vacca, *Memorie di varie antichità*, 36 (Colombo, Rome, 1988).

[5] The precious vase is now in the British Museum.

[6] As mentioned above, it was frequently but erroneously believed that the scenes shown representing mythical events showed the birth of Alexander Serverus.

NECROPOLISES ON THE VIA OSTIENSE

[1] In the area around the basilica of S. Paolo fuori le Mura there was a large necropolis, in use from the end of the Republican era to the fifth century AD, excavated between the end of the nineteenth century and the beginning of the twentieth. While it progressively came to light in the course of road-works carried out there, it is now partly destroyed.

MAUSOLEUM OF ROMULUS

[1] The land on which this complex was built was originally the property of Herodes Atticus (to whom it had come as a dowry after his marriage to Annia Regilla in the second century AD and where he had built his villa).

[2] A. Palladio, *I quattro libri dell'architettura*, I (*I quattro libri dell'architettura*, Hoepli, Milan, 1980).

MAUSOLEUM OF LUCILIUS PETO

[1] The original level was about 6 m. below the present one.

[2] The text reads: V. M. LUCILIUS M. F. SCA. PAETUS TRIB. MILIT. PRAEF. FABR. PRAEF. EQUIT. LUCILIA M. F. POLLA SOROR.

³ It is possible that it was once topped with crenellations.

⁴ The tomb, together with the mound, must have been about 16 m. high.

⁵ It would seem that this type of burial belonged to a later stage in the monument's history, even if not a Christian one.

⁶ A small niche to contain a lamp can often be found near a *loculus*.

MAUSOLEUMS OF S. SEBASTIANO

¹ J. W. Goethe, *Italienische Reise*, III (*Viaggio in Italia*, Rizzoli, Milan, 1991).

² As is often the case with this type of building, it has a series of rooms on two floors arranged around a courtyard.

³ This villa dates from the years 250–240 AD and illustrates the evolution of painting at the time towards a decoration where the early influence of the Pompeian style is reduced to simple linear and geometric motifs.

⁴ The inscription, on the front of the small mausoleum, records that the deceased lived for 75 years and prepared this tomb for himself, his freemen and his descendants. The tomb is arranged on two levels.

⁵ From the name of an association whose members are buried here.

⁶ These themes are echoed in the mosaic pavement, which depicts a family of birds.

⁷ A symbol of immortality, it takes on the specific connotation of resurrection in Christian iconography.

PYRAMID

¹ Traces have been found beneath both of the churches.

² Milanese view of the late fifteenth century.

³ The inscription continues on the eastern side, recording the short time it took to build the monument – 330 days – and the fact that it was placed there in fulfillment of a testamentary wish.

⁴ He, together with his brother, was probably also responsible for the Ponte Cestio that crosses the Isola Tiberina.

⁵ A fine-grained white marble from Luni near Carrara.

⁶ In the third century it was incorporated into the city's defensive system.

⁷ This small opening on the western side was made at the time of the seventeenth-century restoration.

⁸ The funerary chamber measures 5.90 by 4.10 m. and is covered with a barrel vault.

⁹ The decoration consisted of standing or seated figures above a high plinth on which candelabra stood that divided up the spaces. Today, of the four original figures on the walls, some are easier to make out than others.

¹⁰ The vault may have shown an apotheosis, destroyed by robbers in search of valuable grave goods.

COLOMBARIA OF POMPONIUS HYLAS

¹ This is the colombarium of Pomponius Hylas discovered around the middle of the nineteenth century by Marchese Pietro Campana.

² The inscription is placed within a framework of shells where, if one looks closely, the letter V (first letter of *vivit*) can be seen above the name of the woman, indicating that at the time when the inscription was made she was still alive.

³ In fact, the usual structure of a columbarium is only found on one of the walls, that nearest to the stairway. For the rest, the burial place has a highly theatrical architectural arrangement of niches and frontals, leading to the use of the appropriate expression "Roman Baroque" to describe this and similar constructions.

⁴ The naked figure of the youth crowned with vine leaves can be interpreted as *Iacchos*, the mystic hypostasis of *Dionysus*, and is probably connected with the scene below showing the anger of the god who has Orpheus killed as a punishment for having revealed the mysteries. Cf. M. Borda, *La decorazione pittorica del colombario di Pomponio Ila*, Atti Accademia Nazionale dei Lincei, 1947, series VIII, vol I, fasc. 8.

⁵ This is the couple mentioned on a small inscription placed just above lower molding of the niche.

⁶ If details of the technical construction of the columbarium can be dated to the time of Tiberius, the paintings seem to date from a later period, around the second century (cf. the gallery of the Flavians at S. Domitilla).

COLOMBARIA OF VIGNA CODINI

¹ Today there is nothing to see of any of the important discoveries made in the eighteenth century. Even the urns of precious marbles, the jars and an important number of inscriptions have disappeared without trace.

² This columbarium lies to the right, towards the interior of the property. It too dates from the time of Tiberius (lying some 6 m. below ground) and was discovered in 1840 by Marchese Campana.

³ Inside there is a marble relief showing the *dextrarum iunctio* (a husband and wife holding hands) from the Servian period, when the site was no longer used for burials.

⁴ In total, some 500 *loculi* are accessible.

⁵ This columbarium, constructed in *opus reticulatum* and certainly from the Augustan period, lies 7 m. below ground. It was discovered in 1847.

⁶ There are 300 burials.

⁷ The paintings date from slightly later than the construction of the columbarium.

⁸ This columbarium was constructed in the Tiberian period and was in use until the end of the second century. It was discovered in 1852.

⁹ The presence of numerous long slabs of travertine can be explained by the original existence of wooden platforms allowing access to the upper *loculi*.

WATER

¹ According to Orphic genealogy she was the daughter of the Ocean, showing the close connection between nymphs and the watery elements.

NYMPHEUM OF EGERIA

¹ Titus Livy, *Ab Urbe Condita Libri*, I, 21 (*Storia di Roma*, Rizzoli, Milan, 1982).

² Ovid, *op. cit.*, IV, 336.

³ Heriodes Atticus was governor of Asia and Greece. It was said that his father had become very rich from the discovery of an immense treasure on the slopes of the Acropolis, or, more probably, having been a successful speculator.

⁴ It seems that Annia Regilla was expecting her fifth child when she died, her death resulting from a kick.

⁵ Another theory suggests that it was a reference to the sanctuary of Demeter at Cnidos, founded by the king of Thessaly, Triopas. Other scholars relate it to Triope, king of Argos, who was the first to introduce the cult of Ceres-Demeter in Rome.

⁶ One of the surviving buildings is the church of S. Urbano on the Caffarella, beyond the Via Appia Pignatelli. This was once a temple dedicated to the celebration of the goddess Ceres, the deified Empress Faustina, and Annia Regilla.

⁷ Ovid, *op. cit.*, III, 275.

NYMPHEUM OF THE ANNIBALDI

¹ According to Lanciani it was part of the Domus Aurea, but is more likely to have been the remains of a rich *domus*, possibly situated between the top of the Oppian Hill and the *Carinae*, demolished to make way for Nero's great enterprise.

² This nympheum was discovered in 1895 during the construction of the Via Cavour.

³ Countless fragments were discovered during the excavations, which once ornamented the niches. Some pieces of lead piping for the fountains were also found.

AUDITORIUM OF MAECENAS

¹ Discovered in 1874, the *auditorium* of Maecenas consists of a rectangular hall, with an apse on one of the shorter sides. The masonry, where the elements of the *opus reticulatum* are quite small, suggests a date between the end of the Republic and the beginning of the Empire.

² Horace, *Saturae* (*Satire*, Garzanti, Milan, 1976).

³ The hall, partly below ground level even in antiquity, had tubes (later

filled in) in the top step of the *cavea*, from which quantities of water could have flowed. Details such as these have led to the identification of this place as a nympheum.

[4] Orazio, *Odi*, I, 1 (*Odi-Epodi*, Garzanti, Milan, 1986).

[5] The wall paintings belong, in all probability, to the second phase of construction of the building. The decoration is typical of the Third Style, with landscapes and gardens, and was possibly painted at the time of Tiberius when, returning from his voluntary exile in Rhodes, he went to live in Maecenasi villa which, on the death of the original owner, had become part of the imperial domain.

[6] It is not easy to interpret the complex symbolism of these figures, but they are certainly connected with the world of Dionysus and the Bacchantes.

Sacred Places

AREA SACRA OF LARGO ARGENTINA

[1] At some point a curious building was inserted between temples A and B, to serve as the office of water and aqueducts, looked after by the appointed *curator acquarum*.

[2] Three of these alterations were particularly important, taking place between the fourth century BC and the period of Domitian. From being separate units, the temples were brought together into a single and unified place of worship.

[3] Among the various surrounding buildings were a *forica* (latrine), a *hecatostylum* (portico with a hundred columns) and, most importantly, Pompey's *curia*, where Caesar was killed.

[4] Not all temples have underground rooms and passages. Here, only temples C and A have a subterranean area. Temple C has the altar of Aulus Postumius Albinus in its lower rooms. Of particular interest beneath temple A is the superimposition of altars of different periods, and the intricate maze of rooms resulting from the different alterations.

THREE TEMPLES IN THE FORUM HOLITORIUM

[1] Ovid, *Metamorphoson libri* XV, 62–80 (*Le Metamorfosi*, Bompiani, Milan, 1989).

[2] From the word *holus* (vegetables). It was situated in the extreme north of Regio IX (*Circus Flaminius*).

[3] This was a Doric temple, peripteral and hexastyle, with 11 columns on the sides. These are of grayish-white travertine, indicating that they may once have been stuccoed.

[4] With three rows of columns in front and two rows at the back.

[5] With two rows of six Ionic columns in front and eight at the sides (seven on the southern side and two on the north side are still standing).

[6] Pliny, *Naturalis Historia* (*Storia naturale*, Einaudi, Turin, 1985).

[7] On the outer left-hand surface of the basilica it is possible to see the six embedded columns of the Doric temple. Enclosed, but visible, in the right-hand wall are the seven peperino columns of the Ionic temple.

[8] Fra Giocondo, Baldassarre Peruzzi, Antonio and Giovanni Battista da Sangallo, Palladio, and even, it appears, Michaelangelo himself explored the underground areas in order to get a better look at these ancient structures.

[9] The cella over which the nineteenth-century chapel of Our Lady of Guadeloupe now stands was certainly adapted for use as a burial place. The skulls and bones found during excavations have been placed in a small arched niche cut into the wall of the apse on the right.

SYRIAC SANCTUARY ON THE JANICULUM

[1] Today the sanctuary is exposed, and thus cannot be considered subterranean. It is included nevertheless, not so much because it was once underground, but because of its connection with the mystery cults where so much was hidden away and kept secret (cf. Mithraea).

[2] An archaic Italic deity about whom little is known, linked as a chthonic spirit to the underground spring and grove there (*Lucus Furrinae*). At a particular moment her different expressions became fused with the Furrine nymphs.

[3] It is known that the tragic death of Gracchus happened here.

[4] The first period of building dates from the end of the Republic, the second from the Antonine period, and the third, the only one visible today, is generally attributed to the fourth century AD.

[5] It was here that Furrina's sacred spring rose, which was channeled under the temple.

[6] This was Marcus Antonius Gaionas, a rich Syrian merchant, who is mentioned in a number of inscriptions.

[7] In *opus vittatum mixtum*, horizontal blocks of tufa alternating with courses of brick covered with stucco.

[8] This was probably due to a mistake by the architect.

[9] The eggs were broken but, at the moment of discovery, the shells were well preserved, while the content had been emptied over the sculpture. This would appear to confirm the words of Amobius (I, 36) speaking of the Syriac cult: "*ovorum progenies dei Syri*".

[10] This would almost certainly have made up the third component of the Heliopolis triad: Simios, assimilated, through the syncretic pagan religion of the latter years of the Empire, with Adonis, Osiris and Dionysus, with a strong emphasis on resurrection.

[11] The room has an unusual octagonal form and absence of windows (fragments of lamps have been found).

[12] The death and rebirth of the neophyte in symbiosis with that of Nature must certainly have followed an initiatory journey, passing through the seven spheres in a progressive ascent.

S. CRISOGONO

[1] It was a composite building, part of which, a vast hall (in brick, with a monumental facade with arcading), was later converted to Christian use.

[2] The dividing arcades are modern. Those on the right were built to support the left-hand outer wall of the upper church, while those on the left supported the walls of the convent.

[3] The presence of several doors in the perimeter walls have led to suggestions that this building was similar to the so-called iopen basilicasi, such as San Vitale, SS. Giovanni e Paolo, etc.

[4] In fact, such a design has undeniably classical roots (for example, the Servian basilica at Leptis Magna).

[5] G. Mancini, *Rendiconti della Pontificia Accademia di Archeologia*, 1923–1924, pp. 137 ff.

[6] This wall, thought to be eleventh-century, cuts the entire room in two. It bears a fresco with a geometric decoration and a number of arms of the Epifanio family (to which Pope Victor III, who died in 1087, belonged).

[7] This is not found in the martyrologies.

[8] The *titulus* is recorded for the first time in the Roman Council of 499.

[9] The three saints, framed by fluted and twisted columns, are represented standing, richly dressed. They can be identified as St. Chrysogonus, the *vicarius* Rufinus (dressed as a soldier) and St. Anastasia.

[10] These alterations made it possible to excavate a horseshoe-shaped crypt beneath the apse, with two *fenestellae confessionis*, one of which opened onto the corridor placed at right-angles and the other onto the basilica.

[11] In the chamber believed to have been a sacristy, a sarcophagus dating from the second century AD was found. Still closed when found, it had a front panel showing a bust of the deceased and a marine scene with nereids and tritons. Other burials were found, as well as pottery urns for the bodies of children. It is possible that the use of this chamber as a burial place happened at a later date.

[12] These paintings can be dated to the tenth and eleventh centuries AD.

S. CECILIA IN TRASTEVERE

[1] This view is not shared by all scholars. St. Cecilia is venerated as the patron saint of music because, in the above-mentioned *Passio*, we read that *cantantibus organis* (for her wedding) she *decantabat in corde suo*. This does not mean, however, that Cecilia either sang or played.

[2] The basins were later filled in, when the tannery was closed, and covered with a floor of *opus signinum*. The tannery can perhaps be identified with the *Coraria Septimiana* that sources indicate to have been in this area.

[3] This place was built in 1665 for the burial of the nuns. A small museum has been created here with the material found in the course of the excavations.
[4] The work was designed by the architect G.B. Giovenale who, between 1899 and 1901, built the chapel, at the expense of Cardinal Rampolla, the mosaic decorations being carried out by Giuseppe Bravi.

S. CLEMENTE
[1] The *titulus* probably came about from the patrician *domus* of that Clement who was, according to some scholars, a member of the family of the consul and martyr Titus Flavius Clemens and a contemporary of the saint of the same name to whom the church is dedicated.
[2] The text of the dedicatory inscription reads as follows: EGO MARIA MACELLARIA P(RO) TIMORE DEI ET REMEDIO ANIME MEE HEC P(RO) G(RATIA) R(ECEPTA) F(IERI) C(URAVI).
[3] The Slav saints who brought the body of St. Clement to Rome.
[4] Or perhaps a *domus*, the house of a public functionary. Cf. F. Guidobaldi, *San Clemente Miscellany*, IV, 1, Rome, 1992.

S. MARTINO AI MONTI
[1] This theory is not universally accepted.
[2] Their name was indicated according to that of the founders, as the *titulus Pammachii* and the *titulus Vestinae* established (before the fifth century) in accordance with the wills of the senator Pammachius and the matron Vestina.
[3] These dates are debatable, with some scholars suggesting that the building was converted in the fourth century, and others favoring the sixth century.
[4] Fragments of furnishings from the presbytery, including screens, have been found.

SS. GIOVANNI E PAOLO
[1] The *clivus Scauri* is an ancient street that may have connections with the family of the Aemilii Scauri. It starts at the Caelian Gate and gives a very evocative impression of what a late antique street must have been like, with rows of facades on either side and arched passageways.
[2] These were the first religious Christian settlements, generally created from private houses that took on the *titulus* of their owners.
[3] These constructions were gradually uncovered as a result of excavations carried out on the site, beginning in 1887, by Father Germano di San Stanislao and his successors.
[4] The owner may have been the Pammachius or Byzans mentioned in the sources. The church was indeed originally referred to as *titulus Byzantis* or *Pammachii*.
[5] There have been many suggestions as to the number of apartments in the house looking onto the *clivus Scauri*. There may have been one, two, three, four, or even five. According to Krautheimer, there were two. The stratification of the apartments is complicated, dating from different periods with additions and alterations. Since it is difficult to arrive at a definitive answer as far as the construction and phases of these houses is concerned, because of the variety of different theories and because the excavations were never completely finished, the reader is referred to the Bibliography for further information.
[6] Scholars remain undecided about the iconography. The only definite interpretation seems to be the identification of the male figure with Bacchus.
[7] This decoration can be dated to around the second century AD.
[8] There is a basin in this room, while in another room there is a clay one (*labrum*) making it seem likely that there was a private bath complex here.

HYPOGEUM OF THE VIA LIVENZA
[1] This space represents only a small part of the original hall with its rounded structure which is still buried beneath the surrounding buildings. Nevertheless, it represents the most interesting part of the entire complex situated within the vast necropolis of the *Via Salaria Vetus*.
[2] *Inno omerico ad Artemide*, II, 1–10.

[3] R. Paribeni, *Un edificio sotterraneo di tarda età imperiale*, in *Rendiconti della Pontificia Accademia Romana di Archeologia*, 1923; R. Paribeni, *Notizie Scavi*, 1923.
[4] The mosaic is on the right-hand wall, immediately before the large arch that surmounts the paintings.
[5] This theory would seem to be confirmed by the presence here of some brick stamps bearing the monogram of Constantine.
[6] For the most recent research, see G. Wilpert, *Un battistero 'Ad Nymphas B. Petri'*, in *Rendiconti della Pontificia Accademia Romana di Archeologia*, II.
[7] F. Hubaux, *Le plongeon rituel*, in "Musée Belge," XXVII, 1923.
[8] R. Paribeni, *Notizie Scavi*, 1923.

HYPOGEUM OF THE FLAVIANS
[1] Michele Stefano De Rossi is the brother of the better-known Giovanni Battista, father of sacred archaeology.
[2] In 1874 a fragment of an inscription was found by De Rossi in the excavations of the basilica of SS. Nereus and Achilleus. It may have come from the tablet on the facade of the hypogeum. De Rossi completed it to give the following reading: SEPUL(CRUM) FLAVI(ORUM). This reconstruction seems rather approximate and has frequently been questioned.
[3] It was the biggest of the subterranean Roman necropolises arranged on different levels.
[4] The linear style of the pagan paintings makes it likely that they date from the first half of the third century. The Christian paintings, on the other hand, date from the period of the emperor Gallienus (260–268 AD).

INSULAE, DOMUS
[1] Vitruvius, *De Architectura*, II, 8, 17 (*I dieci libri dell'architettura*, SugarCo, Varese, 1990).
[2] See Glossary.
[3] Juvenal, *Saturae*, III, 162–7 (*Satire*, Rizzoli, Milan, 1976).

ROMAN HOUSE BENEATH THE BARRACCO MUSEUM
[1] Thanks to his good relations with the French royal family, he had made the drawing up of the concordat between Leo X and Francois I possible. In recognition of this beneficial act of diplomacy, the king allowed him to add the French lily to his arms. This motif, together with the ermine of Brittany (Le Roy's place of origin) decorates the string-course on the palazzo. Later the lily became confused with the Farnese motif, resulting in the palazzois acquisition of the erroneous name of "Piccola Farnesina."
[2] Some scholars believe that the architect was Antonio da Sangallo the Younger because of a number of similarities of design with the nearby Palazzo Farnese.
[3] The discovery was made at the time of the restoration of the building (1899), when the sixteenth-century facade on Via dei Baullari had to be strengthened.
[4] The majority of the columns were reused ones. Three columns rest on Attic bases that may be compared with constructions of an earlier date, while three others are supported by inverted Tuscan capitals, of very fine quality, also dating from the early Empire.
[5] See Glossary.
[6] The presence of a rectangular marble plinth marks this as a more important area.
[7] The different levels are an indication of the different building phases. The first, with its rectangular slabs of cipollino, is certainly earlier than the construction of the portico.
[8] See Glossary.
[9] Stylistically, these paintings seem to belong to the fourth century.
[10] These measures consist of marble blocks (parallelepiped in form) with, on the upper surface, a number of cavities, generally four (two larger and two smaller in size), corresponding to measures, but without any constants. Metal containers were placed in the cavities and the product for sale (generally cereals) was poured into them.

[11] The scene of the stag hunt was read as a representation of a *desultor*, an acrobat who would leap from one galloping horse to another.

CONSTRUCTIONS BENEATH S. PAOLO ALLA REGOLA

[1] This is the case with the Specchi house at no. 16, Via San Paolo alla Regola, where an intricate palimpsest has been revealed: four stories in height (two of these below ground), the building dating from the Empire later provided the underpinnings for a medieval building.

[2] This floor is now 8 m. below the present street level.

[3] This space, known as "the room of the column," was originally a courtyard open to the sky. An analysis of the masonry has revealed a complex picture of many building phases, with a number of alterations greatly changing the original structure. Rebuilt in the Servian period, two other stores were added, placed in front of the facade of a house. During the period of Constantine, major changes were made when, as a result of a fire, one of the floors was buried and the whole fabric underwent a complete overhaul.

[4] Here too, as with the other courtyard, the historical stratification is very complex.

[5] This use was suggested by the presence of a number of brick basins.

[6] With their own "*Universitas Mercatorum Vaccinorum vel Lanariorum, vel Corariorum.*"

DOMUS AUREA

[1] Suetonius, *De vita duodecim Caesarum libri VIII, VI, XXXI* (*Vite dei Cesari*, Rizzoli, Milan, 1982).

[2] *Roma domus fiet: Veios migrate Quirites, / si non et Veios occupat ista domus.* This is one of the most famous Roman comments on the subject.

[3] Suetonius, *op. cit.*, VI, XXXI.

[4] Pliny, *op. cit.*, XXV, 120.

FUNCTION AND DELIGHT

"*SETTE SALE*"

[1] Despite the continuation of the name, which was given at the time of the original discovery of only seven halls, there are not, in fact, seven.

[2] See Glossary.

[3] The halls are all of the same width (5.25 m.), while the length, decreasing from the center to the sides, ranges from 39.75 to 29.30 m.

[4] The curved form of the back wall corresponded to the precise requirements necessary to sustain the pressure of such a large amount of water.

ROMAN CISTERN IN THE VIA CRISTOFORO COLOMBO

[1] On the walls, which have a brick cladding formed of sesquipedal bricks (45 cm. x 45 cm.), it is possible to see the maker's stamp: TROPHIMI AGATHOBULI / DOMITI TULLI. This can be dated to a period between 93–94 and 108 AD.

[2] Low down, to the right, an irregular opening allows us to see the channel, round in section, where the pipes would have run. The incline of the channel and the point of exit indicate that this was a drain where the waste water ran off.

[3] See Glossary.

AUGUSTAN SUNDIAL

[1] In fact, the obelisk was discovered in the Piazza del Parlamento, near no. 3 and moved in 1748, as can still be read on a plaque installed by Pope Benedict XIV.

[2] Pliny, *op. cit.*, XXXVI, 15, 104–8.

[3] The sundial occupied an enormous area, stretching, from south to north, from the Piazza del Parlamento to the Piazza S. Lorenzo, and, from east to west, between the Via Lucina and the Via della Lupa.

[4] Other remains of the sundial can still be seen beneath the church of S. Lorenzo in Lucina.

STADIUM OF DOMITIAN

[1] The distance of a running race was roughly equivalent to our 200 m.

[2] Suetonius, *op. cit.*, 4, 4.

[3] Since it was a stadium and not a circus, the arena would have had neither *spinae* (on which stood obelisks), nor *carceres* (the starting boxes for the chariots).

[4] Cicero, *Tusculanae disputationes*, IV, 70 (*Toscolane*, Paravia, Turin, 1984).

[5] Tacitus, *Annales* XIV, 20, 4 (*Gli annali*, Garzanti, Milan, 1983).

[6] Seneca, *Epistulae morales*, 80, 2 (*Epistole morali*, Dante Alighieri, Rome, 1990).

[7] The line of the facade consisted of arcades supported by travertine piers with engaged Ionic columns. Between the first and second passageways there was a section made up of piers and radiating walls, into which the stairs were built. From this point travertine takes the place of brick.

[8] The first order had engaged Ionic columns, while the second order was Corinthian.

[9] This was one of the main entrances, in the center of the curved end. There were two other main entrances in the middle of the long sides. Traces of one of these can be seen beneath S. Agnese where, as well as the elements discussed here, the most important remains of the *circus agonalis* are preserved. It is likely that a fourth entrance existed on the south side, in the straight end.

[10] The subterranean area, excavated in 1936–38, has been left visible beneath the INA building. Behind the arcades, on the ground floor, there were three parallel passageways between which there were piers and radial walls that supported the *cavea* and large halls with brick walls interrupted at intervals by the numerous staircases leading to the two superimposed sections of stepped seats.

A LATRINE IN THE VIA GARIBALDI

[1] Strabo, *Geografia*, V, 2, 8 (*Geografia*, Rizzoli, Milan, 1993).

[2] Martial, *Epigrammata*, LXXVII (*Epigrammi*, Garzanti, Milan, 1984).

VII COHORT OF GUARDS

[1] Juvenal, *op. cit.*, III, 192 ff.

[2] *Ibid.*

[3] *Ibid.*

[4] The *praefectus vigilum* had command of some 7,000 men.

[5] Each century consisted of about 100 guards, commanded by a centurion.

[6] This building was 8 m. below the present street level.

[7] It is a small shrine dedicated to the protecting genius of the barracks and must once have been completely covered with frescoes.

[8] This rich collection of graffiti can be dated to the period 214–245 AD.

[9] The *milites sebaciarii* were those whose task it was to prepare the torches (the word *sebaciaria* is derived from *sebum*, meaning "tallow").

[10] Juvenal, *op. cit.*, 272 ff.

Glossary

Aedicule A door, window or niche framed by two columns supported by an entablature and pediment.

Acrolith Wooden statue, clothed, leaving only the extremities uncovered. Arms, head and legs were made of marble, stone or ivory.

Agape Ritual banquet.

Aisle Lateral nave

Ambulatory 1. Covered passage. 2. In medieval churches it is the space where one can pass around the back of the choir.

Apse Hollow construction, semicircular or polygonal in plan, covered with a dome, the interior of which is sometimes called a conch or bowl-shaped vault. Already common in Roman architecture, in Christian churches the central nave and sometimes the side aisles often terminate with an apse.

Atrium 1. The inner space of an Etruscan or Roman house, a sort of courtyard with a portico that gave onto the rooms. 2. In Christian basilicas it was the porti-coed courtyard at the entrance. 3. In a more general sense the word is used to describe the entrance to churches and palaces.

Basilica Roman building intended for public functions, rectangular in plan, sometimes having apses on the side aisles. The Christian church, or basilica, was based on this form.

Cella The innermost part of a temple (corresponding to the Greek *naos*) containing the statue of the divinity venerated there.

Cipollino Marble with parallel stripes, varying from whitish-green to dark green.

Circus Roman construction for chariot racing, typically long with one of the short ends semicircular. Characterized by the presence in the center of the *spina*, a long wall that had at either end a column or obelisk (*meta*), the turning post around which the chariots had to race.

Crypt For the Greeks and Romans, an underground, hidden place. For Christians, the space (or spaces) beneath the presbytery of a church where martyrs were buried.

Cryptoporticus An enclosed gallery having walls with openings instead of columns, typical of Roman architecture. Also a covered or subterranean passage.

Cubiculum 1. The bedroom in a Roman house. 2. In the catacombs, the burial chamber, or *loculus*.

Excubitorium Detachment of guards.

Fistula Water-pipe used in antiquity.

Forum The main square in a Roman city, generally surrounded by colonnades, where the most important public activities took place.

Gnomon Pointer whose shadow indicates the time on a sundial.

Groin (or cross) vault Vault formed by two intersecting barrel vaults resulting in four surfaces.

Hexastyle A temple or building with six columns at the front.

Hypogeum General word for a underground construction.

Mausoleum Large monumental funerary structure. The name is derived from the tomb of Mausolos, king of Caria (350 BC) at Halicarnassus.

Nave Each of the longitudinal spaces into which the interior of a church is divided by means of walls, columns or piers.

Necropolis Cemetery complex.

Obelisk Monolithic pier of eastern origin of a commemorative character.

Odeon Covered building, similar to a small theater, used in antiquity for concerts and musical performances.

Opus reticolatum Walling technique where the surface shows an arrangement of squared stones and bricks placed diagonally in a net-like pattern.

Opus sectile Type of mosaic consisting of slabs of different geomentric shapes generally of marble but sometimes of other materials.

Opus signinum a mixture made up of crushed brick or pottery with sand and lime, used to make floors etc. waterproof.

Opus spicatum Type of Roman masonry made up of stones and bricks arranged in a herringbone pattern.

Opus vittatum Type of Roman masonry made up of horizontal courses of bricks alternating with blocks of tufa, rectangular on the outer surface but tapered to the rear, placed in horizontal bands.

Peperino Tufa of volcanic origin, grayish with flecks.

Peripteral Having a row of columns on all sides.

Peristylium (peristyle) A range of columns surrounded by a building or open court.

Portasanta crushed marble from the eastern Aegean

characterized by spots and veins ranging from pink to blood red on a gray or flesh-colored ground.

Serliana An archway or window with three openings, the central one arched and wider than the others. First illustrated in Sebastiano Serlio's *Architettura* (1537).

Statio Guard house (military).

Tablinum In a Roman house this was the room, situated in the atrium on the side near the entrance, where private documents, family records, etc. were kept.

Travertine Marble from the quarries near Tivoli much used in Roman buildings.

Triclinium Dining room in a Roman house.

Velarium Awning used in theaters in ancient Rome to provide shade for the public and the actors.

Essential Bibliography

U. Bianchi (ed.), *Myteria Mithrae*, Proceedings of the International Conference "La specificità storico-religioso dei misteri di Mithra con particolare riferimento alle fonti documentarie di Roma e di Ostia", Leiden, 1979.

U. Bianchi, *La tipologia storica dei misteri di Mitra* in "Aufstieg und Niedergang der romischen Welt", II, 17, 4, Berlin-New York, 1984.

J. Carcopino, *La vita quotidiana a Roma all'apogeo dell'Impero*, Bari, 1982.

F. Castagnoli, *Tipografia di Roma antica* in *Enciclopedia classica*, III, 10, 3, Turin, 1954.

F. Coarelli, *Guida archeologica di Roma*, Rome, 1974.

L. Crema, *L'architettura romana* in *Enciclopedia classica*, III, 12, 1, Turin, 1959.

F. Cumont, *Textes et monuments figurés relatifs aux mystères de Mithra*, I–II, Brussels, 1896–98.

F. Cumont, *The Mysteries of Mithra*, Dover Publications Inc., 1956.

J. Darmesteter, *Le Zend-Avesta*, Paris, 1892.

I. Della Portella, *Roma Sotterranea: le città sotto la città*, Newton-Compton, Rome, 1996.

Enciclopedia dell'arte antica, Roma, vol. VI, Rome, 1965.

G. Lugli, *I monumenti antichi di Roma e suburbio*, vols I–III and supplements, Rome, 1931–40.

G. Lugli, *Itinerario di Roma antica*, Milan, 1970.

G. Lugli, *Roma antica. Il centro monumentale*, Rome, 1946.

R. Merkelbach, *Mithras*, Konigstein, 1984.

Mithraic Studies. Proceedings of the First International Congress of Mithraic Studies 1971, I–II, Manchester, 1975.

A. Von Prònay, *Mitra*, Florence, 1991.

J.M.C. Toynbee, *Morte e sepoltura nel mondo romano*, Rome, 1933.

C.W. Weber, *Panem et circenses*, Milan, 1989.

SOURCES

Apuleius, *Metamorphóseon libri* XI (*Le Metamorfosi*, Rizzoli, Milan, 1977).

Ausonius, *Epistulae*, XXXI (*Epistole*, Il Cardo, Venice, 1995).

Cicero, *Tusculanae* (*Toscolane*, Paravia, Turin, 1984).

Firmicus Maternus, *De errore profanarum religionum* (*De errore profanarum religionum*, La Nuova Italia, Florence, 1969).

J. W. Goethe, *Italienische Reise* (*Viaggio in Italia*, Rizzoli, Milan, 1991).

Horace, *Carminum libri* (*Odi Epodi*, Garzanti, Milan, 1986).

Horace, *Sermonum libri* (*Satire*, Garzanti, Milan, 1976).

Juvenal, *Saturae,* (Satire, Rizzoli, Milan, 1976).

Justin, *I Apologia* (*Le due Apologie*, Edizioni Paoline, Rome, 1983).

Titus Livy, *Ab Urbe Condita Libri* (*Storia di Roma*, Rizzoli, Milan, 1982).

Macrobius, *Saturnaliorum libri* (*I Saturnali*, UTET, Turin, 1967).

Martial, *Epigrammata* (*Epigrammi*, Garzanti, Milan, 1984).

Orazio, *Odi* (*Odi-Epodi*, Garzanti, Milan, 1986).

Orazio, *Saturae* (*Satire*, Garzanti, Milan, 1976).

Ovid, *Fastorum libri* (*I Fasti*, Zanichelli, Bologna, 1983).

Ovid, *Metamorphoséon libri* (*Le Metamorfosi*, Bompiani, Milan, 1989).

A. Palladio, *I quattro libri dell'architettura* (*I quattro libri dell'architettura*, Hoepli, Milan, 1980).

Plautus, *Mostellaria* (*Mostellaria – Persa*, Mondadori, Milan, 1981).

Pliny, *Naturalis Historia* (*Storia Naturale*, Einaudi, Turin, 1985).

Polybius, *Historiae* (*Storie*, Mondadori, Milan, 1970).

Porphyrius, *De antro nympharum* (*L'antro delle ninfe*, Aldephi, Milan, 1986).

Seneca, *Epistulae morales* (*Epistole morali*, Dante Alighieri, Rome, 1990).

Sallust, *De coniuratione Catilinae* (*La congiura di Catilina*, Mursia, Milan, 1993).

Suetonius, *De vita duodecim Caesarum libri* VIII (*Vite dei Cesari*, Rizzoli, Milan, 1982).

Tacitus, *Annales* (*Gli Annali*, Garzanti, Milan, 1983).

Tertullian, *De Corona* (*De Corona*, Mondadori, Milan, 1992).

Tertullian, *De baptismo* (*De baptismo*, Paravia, Turin, 1968).

Vitruvius, *De Architectura* (*I dieci libri dell'architettura*, SugarCo, Varese, 1990).